THE
CASE FOR
CANCEL
CULTURE
x x x x

THE
CASE FOR
CANCEL
CULTURE

How This Democratic Tool
Works to Liberate Us All

ERNEST OWENS

St. Martin's Press
New York

First published in the United States by St. Martin's Press, an imprint of
St. Martin's Publishing Group

www.stmartins.com

The Library of Congress Cataloging-in-Publication Data is available
upon request.

ISBN 978-1-250-28093-0 (hardcover)
ISBN 978-1-250-28094-7 (ebook)

Our books may be purchased in bulk for promotional,
educational, or business use. Please contact your local bookseller
or the Macmillan Corporate and Premium Sales Department
at 1-800-221-7945, extension 5442, or by email at
MacmillanSpecialMarkets@macmillan.com.

First Edition: 2023

10 9 8 7 6 5 4 3 2 1

To my beloved grandmother, Ethel, who first taught me how to cancel *unapologetically,* and to my dear mother, Lolita, who later taught me how to cancel *with grace*

CONTENTS

X X X X

THE
CASE FOR
CANCEL
CULTURE

X X X X

INTRODUCTION

Why I had to set the record straight on cancel culture.

Amerca is canceled," a friend texted me as news began to roll in on January 6, 2021, that the Capitol Building in Washington, D.C., was under siege by an angry pack of Trump supporters. "They are really trying to take the country back."

Only a day before, social media was noisy with celebration. Progressives were tweeting out excitement over the Democrats winning back the Senate, following runoff victories in Georgia. The Peach State had been flipped from red to blue by a Jewish candidate, Jon Ossoff, and a Black candidate, Rev. Raphael Warnock.

The historic moment was not embraced by all. After months of repeating the big lie that he was the true winner of the election, Trump unleashed a mob of his most rabid followers and urged them to march on the Capitol. Their goal? To insist that Congress and then vice president Mike Pence overturn the election results and name Trump as president. As those domestic terrorists smashed windows and stormed through the Capitol Building, a fearful Congress ducked and ran for shelter. Never in history had

Americans sought to destroy their own capital to flip the results of an election. Sure, there have been disagreements over presidential elections in the past, such as the recount dispute of George W. Bush versus Al Gore or even the outrage over Hillary Clinton losing to Donald Trump despite receiving three million more votes—but something about the 2020 election struck a different nerve. The protesters could simply not accept the reality of the Democratic win, that Joe Biden would be president, with Kamala Harris at his side as the country's first woman of color vice president. The insurrection cost five civilians their lives, many more protesters and police were injured, and four of the officers on duty that day have since died by suicide.

Trump would later be impeached by Congress for a second time for his part in the events of January 6. But perhaps the more consequential reprimand came from social media. After years of tolerating Trump's steady stream of threats and lies, Facebook and Twitter shut down his accounts. It was hardly a display of moral courage, given the end of his term was in sight.

As the world looked on, and with America balanced on the precipice of democracy, I wondered, was my friend right? Was America going to be canceled? By itself? In the end, it was Trump, and not America, who was canceled.

The concept of cancel culture is controversial, yet it's a rare social setting where you don't hear about something or someone being canceled. Celebrities, politicians, movies, foods, toys, even words—all have been canceled, or at least claimed to have been canceled. Right-wing politicians have used cancel culture as a battle cry against progressives, arguing that freedom of speech is under attack by the Left. Progressives who favor it insist that cancel culture is an important tool in holding those who abuse power accountable. Those who remain in the middle, both politically and socially, question whether cancel culture is a nuisance or a necessary action. During the 2021 CPAC conference,[1] whose slogan was "America Uncanceled," Trump declared that "we reject cancel culture!"

Depending on whom you talk to, Chick-fil-A, the chicken-sandwich fast-food company, should be canceled for its problematic stances on LGBTQIA rights. Some might tell you to stop listening to R. Kelly, Chris Brown, Kodak Black, 6ix9ine, Marilyn Manson, and other men in music who have a history of abuse allegations. You may have been warned not to revisit older films such as *Song of the South, Gone with the Wind, Breakfast at Tiffany's,* or classic westerns starring John Wayne because they include racist stereotypes of Black, Brown, and Indigenous people.

Much of the current debate about cancel culture focuses on individuals who are professionally ruined as a result. Society, or some part of it, has found a person's behavior to be unacceptable, and so they are rejected, their future redemption uncertain. Some claim that cancel culture is too harsh, while others say it's simply a form of accountability. The contemporary conversation is mostly about individual people, even though cancel culture has also always touched laws, companies, groups of people, and even countries.

Netflix removed Oscar-winner Kevin Spacey from the hit series *House of Cards* following multiple allegations of sexual assault by the actor. The streaming giant was so committed to scrubbing Spacey from the show, they reworked the final season to completely focus on his character's wife, played by actress Robin Wright. The network's swift cancellation of Spacey allowed the show to create a critically acclaimed conclusion and garner an Emmy.

Who could forget when R&B songstress Chrisette Michele was canceled after she performed during the 2017 presidential inauguration of Donald Trump? Michele, who was a Grammy-nominated artist, lauded by the Black community for her vocals and authenticity, was shunned and considered a traitor by fans who viewed the forty-fifth president as a racist. She told *The Washington Post*[2] that she thought she could "be a bridge" to uniting the country that was still reeling from Trump's 2016 victory. Michele received death threats, suffered a miscarriage from stress, lost a record deal, and had her music rejected by radio stations, among other personal and professional setbacks.

Meanwhile, hip-hop heavyweights such as Kanye West and Lil Wayne backed Trump throughout his infamous presidency, and while they were both criticized by progressives, they continued to achieve commercial success. It's clear that the results of cancellation are anything but consistent. For a myriad of reasons I'll tackle in this book, some weather cancel culture more easily than others.

Before we break down how cancel culture functions, we should go back to the genesis of the phrase. I first heard the word *cancel* used in a new way while enjoying an evening of salacious reality TV in December 2014. The show was VH1's *Love & Hip Hop*, a hilarious look at old and new hip-hop moguls and their frequently twisted love triangles. And Black Twitter loved to weigh in on the drama and gossip in real time. I love live tweeting television. There is nothing quite like seeing people around the world share similar or opposing views on the same show at the same time.

In this episode, music producer Cisco Rosado was confronted at a restaurant by his love interest at the time, Diamond Strawberry. Strawberry had left her life behind to follow Rosado to New York and was frustrated that he was keeping her a secret from his friends. She revealed to him during lunch that she had a child and that she wanted them to live as a family. Strawberry was combative and began to raise her voice. Rosado started to signal he was breaking up with her. Worried that she was losing her man—and possibly her clout—she told him she wasn't going anywhere. Drinks splashed; glasses shattered.

And then, Rosado gave her the two-word dismissal[3] that might just have started a revolution: "You're canceled."

After that, Black Twitter couldn't get enough of the phrase, and many used it for both serious and silly issues. Ed Sheeran was canceled for calling the VMA's race argument between Taylor Swift and Nicki Minaj at the time "redundant." Amy Schumer was canceled on social media for racist jokes she'd made in the past. Friends canceled each other for liking bizarre foods. My husband told me I would get canceled if I didn't stop buying iceberg lettuce. In Philadelphia, where I live, people began to cancel those who liked certain cheesesteaks over others.

Rosado would later admit that he picked up the phrase from Wesley Snipes's character in *New Jack City,* a film he happened to watch the night before taping that now iconic scene. In the movie, Snipes's character, Nino Brown, breaks up with his girlfriend and declares, "Cancel that bitch. I'll buy another one." Bizarre as it may seem, cancel culture started as a catchphrase poached from a misogynist film clip, but it has taken up its own unique identity.

Since Rosado's "cancel" outburst in 2014, the meaning of canceling quickly evolved. Black social media users were the first to employ the term, but like all things embraced by Black people, the trend would eventually catch mainstream attention. In the crossover process, the concepts of being "canceled" and being "called out" began conflating. Callout culture gained traction[4] on social media in the early 2010s thanks to Tumblr blogs like *Your Fave Is Problematic* and other online discussions about questionable behavior from public figures. Back then, the concept was simple: Powerful people and things that had flaws must be called out, both to bring attention to and to correct said behavior. Tone-deaf tweets, inappropriate photos, phone recordings, screenshots, and other documented foul play by well-known people were distributed by the public as a callout. Eventually, people started using the term *cancel* in place of saying *callout* as they became emboldened to move from simply highlighting bad behavior to acting against it.

The shift from callout to cancellation has certainly created complications. If someone is canceled, are they gone forever, as the word suggests? The mutability of the concept of cancel culture has allowed different people to bend its meaning to their will. And that's why the conversation around cancel culture needs to be more nuanced than it currently is. I believe cancel culture is about being able to speak truth to power. Does that mean people in power can't take cancel culture out for a spin? It's not that simple.

Although cancel culture is not exclusively the purview of my own generation of millennials and Gen Zers, we have redefined how effective cancel culture can be. We were the ones who moved the needle on social media by calling for more law enforcement accountability and racial justice via #DefundThePolice. The extrajudicial killing of George Floyd in 2020 inspired many of us to collectively cancel racist institutions and demand divestment from them. It wasn't enough to just declare such police policies as problematic, but to apply pressure to see them terminated. The difference between cancel culture and callout culture is that while the latter just simply states the problem, the former acts to eradicate it. Of course, #DefundThePolice has become a complicated debate, in the way that cancel culture debates often do. Conservatives were quick to use the phrase to paint progressives as extremists who would make Americans less safe. In response to activism around policing, many cities, such as Oakland, San Francisco, and Durham, increased police budgets by putting extra funds toward alternative supports, such as social workers and civilian responders.

This same younger generation is mobilizing on social media to protest homophobia, transphobia, and other forms of discrimination. During the summer of 2021, rapper DaBaby faced ongoing calls to be canceled from music concerts and other appearances following an anti-LGBTQIA and HIV-phobic rant during a performance at the Rolling Loud music festival. His fan base, which is predominantly millennial and Gen Z, took to Twitter and other social media outlets to condemn his remarks and urged the entertainment industry at large to not support his career until further notice. He quickly lost gigs, like Lollapalooza and the UK's Parklife festival.

Moments like these highlight how cancel culture represents not only a new digital form of protest, but also a promising way for progressives to create change in real time. Whereas anyone and everyone can cancel, not all choose to use such a timely tool to make a positive impact. Cancel culture is nuanced, subjective, and highly accessible. Just like a gun, it can either be viewed as a form of protection or a weapon of terror. Cancel culture has emboldened a younger generation of people to speak truth to power. In the hands of conservatives, it has also reinforced entrenched power structures that weaponize privilege against the marginalized. I've experienced firsthand the ways that cancel culture can be used both for the greater good, and to harass and bully.

My first personal run-in with cancel culture was in June 2016, during the BET Awards. I love live tweeting, and as a pop culture watchdog and freelance journalist covering racial injustice, I never missed the BET Awards. Actor Jesse Williams went viral that night with his Humanitarian Award acceptance speech defending Black Lives Matter, giving voice to a generation of activists who felt misunderstood by mainstream media. Like many others, I was quick to praise Williams. Then entered Justin Timberlake,[5] inserting himself in what was a Black Twitter moment with a tone-deaf attempt to join the conversation. Speaking in African American Vernacular English (AAVE), Timberlake tweeted out: "Jesse Williams tho . . . #Inspired."

I can still remember how annoyed I was. Here was Timberlake, who has a long history of appropriating the musical stylings and aesthetics of Black artists, "inspired" yet again by a Black man who was calling out the exploitation of Black creators. Timberlake and his "blue-eyed soul" benefited from a racist system that prioritized white artists who perform R&B over Black artists who invented the genre. Timberlake and many others wouldn't have reached such career heights had it not been for their mix of talent, white privilege, and the racist industry that favors them. Maybe this would be the moment he would speak up about his white privilege? Would he take ownership for his part in the racism Williams was speaking about? And would this be the moment he finally acknowledged how his whiteness protected him from facing the same scrutiny Janet Jackson experienced over a decade ago during their infamous 2004 Super Bowl halftime show "Nipplegate"? After that so-called wardrobe malfunction, Jackson faced slut-shaming and industry blackballing, while Timberlake played the role of the innocent victim. Only a week after that scandal, Timberlake accepted a Grammy award for Best Male Pop Vocal Performance for his hit "Cry Me a River." Jackson was banned from attending.

Taking all of that into consideration, I felt like it was fair to call Timberlake out on how "inspired" he was. I wanted to know if, years later, he felt any remorse for his actions. Short answer: Not at all. My tweet: "So does this mean you're going to stop appropriating our music and culture? And apologize to Janet too." Rather than respond, Timberlake dodged my questions altogether and chose to condescendingly refer to me as a "sweet soul."

"Oh, you sweet soul," he tweeted back at me. "The more you realize that we are the same, the more we can have a conversation. Bye."

I read his response as both homophobic, given my public profile as a Black queer journalist, and a bit of Southern shade, along the lines of "bless your little heart." Either way, his all-lives-matter "we are the same" response, followed by a "bye" made it clear to me that he had no time to engage in a genuine conversation about racism in the music industry.

In true Timberlake fashion, he immediately made himself out to be the victim of our exchange. Instead of apologizing to Janet or addressing the issues raised in my tweet, he replied that he had "responded to a specific tweet that wasn't meant to be a general response" and how he "shouldn't have responded anyway."

In that instant, Twitter exploded. Notifications were so heavy, the Twitter app on my phone became inactive. I went to my laptop, and it was as real as I'd anticipated. Timberlake had fifty-five million Twitter followers at the time, and they were the only ones I could spot in my notifications at first. I was called out by name, and threats were coming in by the dozens. Folks with fewer than twenty followers and no profile picture felt bold enough to hurl racist and homophobic replies. I was being bullied for my own attempt to call out Timberlake.

That was the point I went off. I wasn't going to sit back and take it. I told Timberlake how condescending he was to whitesplain my legitimate concerns. He never did reply to my other tweets, and by then, he was trending worldwide on Twitter for his initial clapback. Black Twitter came to the rescue and had my back. Suddenly, my timeline was full of images of JT in cornrows or rocking bandannas, and YouTube clips of his collaboration with Timbaland and Nelly Furtado, called "Give It to Me," where he has the audacity to diss Prince.

The next morning, the media outlets began covering the exchange, with many framing me as a villain for being too hard on Timberlake and questioning whether it was fair to accuse him of cultural appropriation. Charlemagne tha God of *The Breakfast Club* used their in-house wrist-slap segment to make me and others who criticized Timberlake on Twitter "Donkey of the Day." Whoopi Goldberg defended the pop superstar on *The View* by saying that "we all appropriate." My tweets were featured across various news outlets—even *The Daily Show*—and many of them refused to so much as name me or state that they came from a legitimate journalist.

I began to see how Timberlake's "oblivious do-gooder" routine manipulated the narrative to his benefit. I got framed as the loud Black guy on Twitter trying to start shit, while he became the hero who took on a Twitter mob. If white fragility had a face, Justin Timberlake was it. He'd bring up our infamous Twitter exchange again in 2018 while promoting his folksy *Man of the Woods* album. Talking to journalist Zane Lowe[6] of Beats 1, he doubled down on his victimhood. "I felt terrible, you feel terrible," Timberlake lamented our online fight, "like, 'Oh man, that is not what I meant. Why did I do that?'"

It would not be until February 2021 that some level of vindication would arrive in the form of a curated apology on social media. "Did you see this?" several of my friends, followers, and family messaged me. "He finally did it." Of course I knew. Google alerts had notified me the moment it happened. The popular documentary *Framing Britney Spears*[7] portrayed Timberlake and his treatment of his ex-girlfriend in a particularly bad light.

Justin Timberlake took to Instagram to apologize not only to her but also to another entertainment heavyweight that he's disparaged over the years: Janet Jackson. "I've seen the messages, tags, comments and concerns and I want to respond," he wrote in the post, speaking of how his "missteps" contributed to "a system that condones misogyny and racism." He went on, "I am deeply sorry for the times in my life where my actions contributed to the problem, where I spoke out of turn, or did not speak up for what was right."

Oh, cry me a river. The damage had already been done. What seemed like petty callout culture at first led to Timberlake eventually admitting his wrongdoings, and a wider cultural discussion about the double standards when it came to Janet Jackson's and Britney's treatment. It obviously took years—and some bad publicity in the form of a Britney Spears documentary—for Timberlake to own up to his bad behavior. Was he truly repentant, or was his hand forced? Whatever was in his heart, Timberlake was forced by cancel culture to acknowledge that his previous actions were out of step with the current climate. It may have taken a long time for consequences to catch up to Timberlake, but it's certainly a positive and satisfying example of cancel culture in action.

Throughout my career, I've wrestled with what it means to call people out and, in turn, be called out, sometimes by powerful individuals and institutions. As my social media accounts began to be verified (a blue check on Facebook, Twitter, and Instagram can both help legitimize your presence and make you a target) and my media content gained traction in the public eye, I was no longer just the source of information but sometimes the news itself. Before my Twitter beef with Timberlake, I only had a little over two thousand followers on Twitter and no verification to make me anyone the public should bother knowing. I think that's part of the reason why Timberlake chose to pick on me in the first place—because he had over fifty-five million followers that he presumed would back him up against my smaller following. It was a David-versus-Goliath scenario that backfired on him quickly. This would not be the last time someone would attempt to silence me online, particularly as I waded into deeper waters than just pop culture beefs.

And this is what many people who hold positions of power and influence misunderstand about cancel culture.

Yes, powerful people can wield cancel culture against those below them, but they can be targets, too. Before the advent of social media, the Timberlakes of the world reached fans through concerts, TV interviews, magazine spreads—all platforms that can be manipulated by celebrities and their PR teams. Social media has made celebrities more accessible to their fans but also more vulnerable to pushback. As they say, everyone's a critic.

My experience with Timberlake caused me to think more deeply about the distinctions between cancel culture and straight-up bullying. Of course, I felt bullied by Timberlake's legion of fans coming after me. Ad hominem attacks—which is what were hurled against me—aren't cancel culture. Timberlake may have felt like he was defending his right to free speech, and I was simply collateral damage. I'd learn that these phenomena are interconnected. If you explore cancel culture and the actions that inspire it, you're sure to experience bullying. Rest assured, throughout the book, I'll discuss the difference.

In my case, the most extreme example[8] had me hauled into a police station for what I call *Facebooking while Black*. In Philadelphia, there is a long history of New Year's Day parades of Mummers—elaborately costumed dancers with a well-known racist, transphobic history. It's an event that divides Philadelphians, largely along sociopolitical lines. I have written several pieces criticizing the Mummers and, on this occasion, wrote a shaming post on Facebook. In this act, I was partaking in cancel culture—inviting people to think differently and take the action of not supporting the Mummers Parade. One of its members found my post threatening enough that he went to the police with his fear, and that was enough to have me brought in and questioned for hours. It's no secret that Black men get treated with high levels of suspicion by police. So when a white person brings the police into a situation with a Black man, it's an all-out act of aggression. This man was not wielding cancel culture against me, he was bullying me.

As I dealt with the trauma of having been interrogated, an internal conflict intensified. Every piece of media content I created, I over-questioned. Every social media post I wrote required a deep breath before publishing. Even if nothing was said to me directly, I felt like I was walking on thin ice on the very social media platforms that gave me visibility. I began to assess how much of myself I gave up on social media. I also began questioning the point of calling people out online if those with privilege and power—usually the ones I was criticizing—could easily manipulate the narrative and retaliate against me. And that's a key weapon of the bully—to have his or her victims police themselves.

None of these events occurred in a vacuum. Place these experiences against a backdrop where bullying is on the rise across the board. The election of Trump emboldened a culture of toxic hostility toward minorities. In 2019, *The Washington Post*[9] reported that counties that had hosted a 2016 Trump campaign rally saw a 226 percent increase in hate crimes over comparable counties that did not host such rallies. The Left is not perfect when it comes to bullying. The Democratic primary season was rife with controversy over the tactics of Bernie Sanders's most passionate followers, infamously known as Bernie Bros. Sanders's political opponents—and even organizations that didn't agree with all his policies—received threatening phone calls, as well as online trolling.

Given how much time we spend on screens, much of this bullying is happening online. According to a 2019 report from the Cyberbullying Research Center, over 36 percent of people feel they have been cyberbullied in their lifetimes—more than double what was reported a decade ago. And it's only getting worse. The report also stated that 87 percent of young people have seen cyberbullying in their lifetimes. It's an alarming statistic, given the Pew Research Center findings[10] that 95 percent of teens are connected to the internet, with 85 percent of them being social media users.

While everyone can agree that cyberbullying—or any kind of bullying—is wrong, it's been all too easy for people to paint cancel culture as a form of bullying. Frequently, people who are being canceled will claim they are being bullied. And some who bully may claim they are canceling. Bullying is rooted in causing deliberate harm, nothing more. Cancel culture is rooted in causing transformative change—something more is being demanded.

Clarity on my own stance on cancel culture came from a surprising source. Former president Obama was giving a speech[11] at an Obama Foundation event. "This idea of purity and you're never compromised, and you're always politically 'woke' and all that stuff," he said. "You should get over that quickly. There are ambiguities. People who do good stuff have flaws. People who you are fighting may love their kids. And share certain things with you." He went on to shade what he seemed to be framing as a new method of holding people to account. "The way of me making change is to be as judgmental as possible about other people and that's enough? That's not activism," Obama declared. "That's not bringing about change. If all you're doing is casting stones, you're probably not going to get that far. That's easy to do."

Two things happened at that moment: Everything clicked, and I lost it. Obama, the man I had so admired growing up, had completely misunderstood what this was all about. And somewhere along the way, I had, too. I got distracted by the events in my own life and allowed them to cloud my thoughts on cancel culture. Something about the way the forty-fourth president of the United States had dismissed the work of millennials and Gen Zers didn't sit well with me. Here he was having an interview with actress Yara Shahidi about youth activism for his summit and not reading the room at all. In seeing how he mischaracterized our motivations, our purpose, and our impact, I could also see how cancel culture was so effective. In my op-ed debut in *The New York Times*[12] in November of 2019 with a piece titled "Obama's Very Boomer View of 'Cancel Culture,'" I argued that "old, powerful people often seem to be more upset by online criticism than they are by injustice." The heated reaction from moderates and boomers alike only confirmed my new understanding. Of course, those in power are eager to write off cancel culture as reckless—they're the ones being canceled.

In the debate over cancel culture, comedians, celebrities, and politicians invoke slippery slopes, arguing that nothing will be safe or sacred if people choose to "cancel" everything they take offense to. It's ironic that those in power, like Obama, are saying that the less powerful can be harmful in their attempts to speak truth to power. Sounds like fearmongering to me. Why don't they want people calling out behaviors and actions? What are they afraid of?

One of the biggest protests against cancel culture came in the summer of 2020, when a legion of over 150 public figures signed an open letter published by *Harper's Magazine*[13] denouncing the "restriction of debate." "Editors are fired for running controversial pieces; books are withdrawn for alleged inauthenticity; journalists are barred from writing on certain topics," the letter, signed by people such as J. K. Rowling, Noam Chomsky, Gloria Steinem, and Malcolm Gladwell, cried. "Professors are investigated for quoting works of literature in class; a researcher is fired for circulating a peer-reviewed academic study; and the heads of organizations are ousted for what are sometimes just clumsy mistakes."

It wasn't only journalistic or academic realms that felt under fire. Conservative blogger Matt Walsh had words for the rising protests against sexual assault. "The #MeToo movement does not facilitate a thoughtful discussion about sexual assault," he wrote in a piece published in the Daily Wire[14] titled "It's Time for the #MeToo Movement to End." He said, "It impedes the discussion. Prohibits it. That's how hysteria always works. The hysterical mob demands your unthinking participation. It does not want to answer any questions or entertain any rational critiques. It is not interested in subtlety or nuance. You must jump on the Bandwagon of Outrage or be trampled underneath it." (Walsh conveniently ignores the fact that he wouldn't likely be talking about sexual assault if not for the #MeToo movement.)

That "Bandwagon of Outrage" was, of course, a dog whistle against cancel culture. The most powerful and influential were basically telling us: "Enough." What some consider standing up for what you believe in, others find to be "a vogue for public shaming and ostracism," according to the open letter published by *Harper's Magazine*.

Cancel culture is more than simply heated debates on social media, but a culture war of the most epic proportions—which is why the social elite try to suppress the everyday person's way of protesting. In doing this, they also try to play the victim and make us the oppressor. I realized that the cart was being put before the horse, by faulting people who were calling out problematic behavior rather than discussing the behavior itself. Did any of them ever try to push back on how the actions of those in power had adversely impacted those with less power? The short answer is no. The mainstream narrative suggests that both parties involved in cancel culture begin on equal footing. This misapprehension allows the powerful to be treated as victims.

Hearing these debates infuriated me. Here I was, second-guessing how I showed up on social media, and the very powerful were pretty much shaming me for defending myself. But I'd soon get a chance to present my understanding of cancel culture. In the fall of 2020, I made an appearance on the popular YouTube show called *Blakademik*.[15] The international show features Black voices from across the African diaspora. The episode I was invited to was titled "The Problem with Cancel Culture." The other guests were writer Chiedza Matsvai, who didn't believe cancel culture existed, and YouTube personality Options Gang Karl, who claimed to have nearly canceled himself.

Throughout the discussion, Karl and I were at each other's throats. Karl suggested that cancel culture was driven by a mostly progressive social media who simply wanted to ruin the livelihoods of people they disagreed with. He argued that some of the historical figures we admire today would have not been able to succeed if cancel culture existed then.

"Malcolm X could not exist by y'all standards today," Karl argued. "Detroit Red could not go through that transition and become Malcolm X." In other words, Karl was saying that if Twitter existed in the 1960s, Malcolm X would have been canceled by MLK followers who disagreed with his political stances, therefore robbing us of what he had to contribute to the culture.

I pushed back on his assertion, making the argument that cancel culture isn't simply a dispute of personal beliefs but that it speaks truth to power. If we look at Karl's Malcolm X argument, it does not hold up. If people had trolled Malcolm X in this imaginary past, that would not have been cancel culture. If they had made legitimate critiques about his politics or methods, it might have been. Critics like Karl often interpret cancel culture incidents as personal attacks rather than challenging institutional pushbacks on social media. They fall down the rabbit hole of looking at problematic behavior as matters of opinion, rather than legitimate offenses.

For example, when comedian Dave Chappelle faced backlash[16] in the fall of 2021 for making a series of transphobic jokes during his Netflix special *The Closer,* his fans argued that he was simply being funny and claimed that those demanding that the episode be removed from the streaming platform were proving his point by trying to cancel him. Many LGBTQIA advocacy groups called for Netflix subscribers to boycott the special in protest. "It's just making jokes. That doesn't mean hate," firebrand media personality Joe Rogan said of Chappelle's controversy[17] during an October 2021 episode of his popular podcast, *The Joe Rogan Experience.* "This is the problem with today: If you don't have an enemy, you make an enemy. And this is a real problem with people. We look for things."

Why was Rogan so quick to come to Chappelle's defense? Were birds of a feather flocking together? Rogan, who has received his fair share of online condemnation for his racist, transphobic, and anti-vaccination rhetoric, is no stranger to cancel culture himself.

Back to me and Karl: When asked why he'd been canceled, Karl stammered, "It was something like jokes on dark-skin girls, but I couldn't remember. I'm an equal opportunity distributor."

In fact, he admitted he'd made offensive remarks about dark-skinned women on Twitter during his stint on the hit YouTube show *The Grapevine,* which caused producers of the show to remove him. He also admitted that Twitter later permanently suspended his account due to his violation of the company's rules "against abuse and harassment" in another incident. In other words, a man who was actively toxic was angry about cancel culture.

It may seem like cancel culture is new, but this is simply the latest manifestation of an ongoing battle between the oppressed and the oppressor that we've witnessed throughout history. When American colonists dumped tea into the ocean during the Boston Tea Party and refused to be taxed without representation—that was cancel culture. Black people refusing to ride in segregated buses in Montgomery, Alabama—that was cancel culture. The boycotting of South Africa to end apartheid in that country— cancel culture. Long before there was social media and viral hashtags, boycotts and demonstrations were cancel culture by another name.

Cancel culture is a modern form of protest that incorporates social media and individualized action—from former quarterback Colin Kaepernick taking a knee during the national anthem to protest police brutality that inspired #TakeAKnee to other hashtags trending on social media worldwide, including one asking music fans to #MuteRKelly for his longtime sexual misconduct. Early practitioners of cancel culture online were quick to realize the power of hashtag slogans in spreading their messages.

Cancel culture can also be a way of remedying past events. In 1985, Philadelphia officials authorized a bomb to be dropped in the Osage Avenue section of West Philadelphia in a standoff with a radical Black activist group called MOVE. The incident sparked international headlines, then and now, as no major American city had ever done something as lethal to its own civilians since the civil rights movement of the 1960s. For decades, politicians and community members debated whether it was acceptable for the MOVE bombing to happen. In 2020, many residents shamed the city of Philadelphia on social media and applied pressure on them to formally apologize for previously bombing a Black neighborhood that killed eleven people, including five children. Of course, an apology doesn't undo the harm caused, but cancel culture can help provide a small sense of justice.

Today, Black Lives Matter activists are demanding that we defund the police and not support elected officials who aren't protecting Black communities. The #MeToo movement is asking that we no longer stay silent and allow those in power to abuse and victimize innocent people. It's not about just calling institutions out but about calling for change in more direct and digital ways. Cancel culture is about making offenders aware of the impact of their actions on social media and beyond.

It's become clear that we risk having the term *cancel culture* hijacked by the very people who most fear being canceled. Shouldn't that make us question how the powerful frame cancel culture? Cancel culture gives individuals who do not have institutional, social, or cultural power a platform to hold those in power accountable. Twitter was a platform for me to confront Justin Timberlake for his many years of cultural appropriation. Social media and documentary film were the outlets for Black women and girls to finally make the world take seriously the predatory actions of convicted sex offender R. Kelly.

I would not have been able to marry my male college sweetheart if it weren't for the radical queer and transgender activists who rioted in the streets to cancel police-sanctioned bigotry at Stonewall. Cancel culture is what has given me, a Black queer millennial, the freedoms that so many take for granted. Before we called it *canceling*, we called it *taking a stand, speaking truth to power, saying it like it is, giving power to the people,* and *making sure that the revolution would not be co-opted.* Cancel culture is the new digital wave of individualized protest and a way to demand change in a society that has yet to grant liberation to all. While previous iterations of protest and public outcry were more traditionally coordinated, in person, and institutional, cancel culture is more personal and is carried out on social media. Such online combativeness from individuals speaking their truth to power is unlike anything we've ever witnessed, because cancel culture invites us all to fight back—a consequential feat and rare opportunity that social media has given us at a time when we need it the most.

I wrote this book to reveal how the essence of cancel culture has impacted our lives long before it became a buzzworthy term. Too often, we treat such trendy terms as fleeting phenomena—matters that can easily be disposed of and forgotten. But that can't be said of cancel culture. From the beginning of society, humans were given the ability to make choices. At the most basic level, the origins of cancel culture began at that moment—the ability to make decisions and express dissent has been key to our very existence. By deciding what we stand for, we also decide what we won't stand for. Our decisions are statements about what stays and what goes. Cancel culture hasn't gone anywhere, and it won't if people exist.

In this book, I will explore the history, complexities, and identity politics shaping cancel culture and why it's more complicated than just some viral social media moments. Why should we care? Because in a world where protest and free speech are being challenged by the most powerful institutions, we deserve to understand the nuance and importance of cancel culture. Those who actively seek to obstruct the diversity, inclusion, and equity we should all be striving for shouldn't have the final say in what gets canceled or not. Rather than seeing cancel culture as a nasty by-product of the digital age, it should be seen as a powerful tool for change. And don't be fooled by people equating all bullying with cancel culture. People behave badly, especially online, and nobody wants to be on the receiving end of hateful messages from online trolls. But cancel culture is not bullying—it's a call for accountability. One should walk away from this exploration not despising cancel culture but embracing it as a form of democratic expression that's always been leading the charge in liberating us all.

The case for cancel culture is simple: Our way of life has, and forever will, require it.

CANCEL CULTURE BEEN HERE

X X X X X X X X X X X X X X X

Before it was called *cancel culture:* The protests, boycotts, and enforcements of political correctness that have taken place throughout history are solid proof that this is not a new phenomenon.

One of the biggest misperceptions about cancel culture is that it is some new, diabolical trend that's upending everyday life. Politicians, celebrities, and mainstream media have framed cancel culture as an out-of-the-box approach they've never seen before. Various generations have pointed the finger at social media as the instigator of cancel culture and swear up and down that things were different back in their day.

"These kids, it's unbelievable," said hip-hop mogul Jay-Z during an April 2021 interview[1] with *The Sunday Times,* sharing his thoughts on cancel culture. "I feel a bit sorry for the younger stars coming up today."

A rapper in his fifties, Jay-Z suggested that cancel culture is behind his decision to use social media infrequently. "Imagine having a microphone, and you're asked about social justice questions at 18 years old," he said. "It's like, 'What?' I'm meant to know the answer, and if

I don't answer the correct way, if I don't say everything right, even if my intentions are right, and I don't say the same right thing, it's going to be everywhere.'"

If only cancel culture was that black and white. Jay-Z's myopic hot take shows how little time he spends on social media and does more to fearmonger than to clarify the current climate. *Which famous eighteen-year-olds are being asked social justice questions they don't know anything about? What's the "correct way" to answer? Who got canceled for an innocently fumbled interview?*

What makes this position on cancel culture problematic is that it is falsely framed as a generational crisis, rather than a reflection of ongoing issues. Listening to Jay-Z, one would believe that future thinkers and creators are bound to be under attack, unlike older individuals, like himself, who are immune to cancel culture because they don't tweet or do many interviews. This faulty logic, rooted in ageism and paternalism, suggests two things: first, that social media is something being used mostly by millennials and Gen Z; second, that cancel culture is only targeting younger people who are impressionable, imperfect, and innocent. While it's true that different age groups gravitate to different platforms, every age group uses some form of social media and most of the high-profile examples of cancel culture have impacted older adults. *Which eighteen-year-olds got canceled, Jay? Do you mean Harvey Weinstein, R. Kelly, and Bill Cosby?* Jay-Z once rapped what would become one of his most signature verses: "Men lie, women lie, numbers don't." He should heed his own advice here. If he did, he'd have to concede that the majority of those being canceled are people and institutions with power and influence. This framing of cancel culture as new is also being carried out by the press. In 2020, *Liberty Champion,* the official student newspaper of Liberty University, ran an op-ed[2] titled "Social Media Is Overrun by Cancel Culture," with a writer claiming at the time that "2020 has been and still is a year full of division and controversy as cancel culture continues to thrive on social media and even in the workplace." An NBC News story on cancel culture[3] in 2019 defined it by saying "the social media phenomenon that takes user outrage and transforms it into a large-scale rejection of a celebrity's work, product or place in pop culture—has affected a variety of celebrities in a wide range of situations in the last year."

Cancel culture isn't new at all. In fact, its genesis is far from the modern confines of social media and celebrity takedowns. The ethos of cancel culture has been here since the beginning of time and is deeply ingrained in our historical fabric. Boycotts, censorships, petitions, social media calls for resignations, and protests are some of the major elements that fuel cancel culture. To treat this current era of accountability as being something new is intellectually dishonest. You don't get America, its Constitution, civil rights, women's rights, LGBTQIA rights, parental advisory stickers on CDs, or other democratic expressions without cancel culture. Regardless of changes in its aesthetic presentations over time, cancel culture's core is accountability.

On the most basic level, the definition of the term *cancel* is simply "to end," but this shouldn't be confused with the term *cancel culture*. Humans choosing to reject something or someone has been as essential to our existence as breathing. Such actions aren't automatically cancel culture, but choosing to reject something because you believe it fundamentally impacts your way of life—is. For example, when millions of Americans elected Joe Biden as U.S. president in 2020, they were also canceling the reelection bid of incumbent Donald Trump simultaneously. This was an act of cancel culture because the decision was rooted in a voter's sociopolitical beliefs. Not all votes are examples of cancel culture—but in the case of Joe Biden versus Donald Trump, people truly felt like a way of life was at stake. Boycotts against companies that discriminate against people is cancel culture. A person not liking a company because they have an ugly logo isn't. Cancel culture is about substance, not style.

Humans are complex, nuanced, and often contradictory when it comes to making decisions—even when it comes to canceling. The rationale behind why we choose to partake in cancel culture varies by political view, religion, desire, time, place, money, status, class, education level, race, gender, sexuality, nationality, and age, among other factors. As a result, canceling means different things to different people, which is why it can show up in different ways, depending on power dynamics.

For example, in ancient, colonial, and imperialistic eras, those with power dominated the narrative. Those with money, authority, and weaponry got to do whatever they wanted with unchecked intimidation. Just like God, those who held the power felt entitled to define what was just and what was law. Religion instilled a sense of blind allegiance and obedience that was carried out in modern lawmaking and policy. The wages of defiance were often death or imprisonment, which bred submission. Back in those days, being hanged, scalped, killed, enslaved, or exiled for protesting were widely accepted forms of being canceled by those who reigned supreme. At the time, the most powerful felt they were holding those accountable for threatening their way of life. While there were tales of revolts and rebellions, many often ended in bloodshed. For example, Joan of Arc was canceled by being burned at the stake in 1431. She was considered a defiant, cross-dressing heretic who claimed God told her to attack the English. Her execution was a textbook example of cancel culture by a church court in a pre-democratic society. There are some people out there bellyaching today that might consider themselves lucky that their reputations, not their lives, have been wiped out as a result of cancellation.

Of course, guns, germs, and steel gave advantages to those who abused their power. For example, the early rise of white supremacy via the Spanish conquistadors invading the Aztecs, the prevalence of Christian Crusades, and the transatlantic slave trade allowed for the end of other civilizations. White colonists took over America with gun power and were determined to cancel what they thought were the barbaric ways of Native Americans in order to form what they considered to be "the New World." This racist superiority complex inspired the nineteenth-century doctrine of manifest destiny, which was the idea that white people had a divine right to expand their control of American land that wasn't theirs. This entitlement, furthered by explorers such as Lewis and Clark, robbed Indigenous peoples of their agency and property. America—to those white colonialists—was theirs for the taking, either through faith, self-declaration, or war. These actions were early examples of cancel culture because these individuals relied on canceling other civilizations to advance their own livelihoods—even if it caused harm to others. Over the course of this book, I'll show how cancel culture evolved from this to be something that is overwhelmingly a force for good today.

IN THE BEGINNING

Canceling is essentially saying no. "No, that is not acceptable to me, or us, this organization, this country, or even, this divine being." According to Abrahamic religions, the first no happened in the Garden of Eden when God essentially banned Adam and Eve from the premises after they violated his request not to eat the forbidden fruit. Such a rejection and condemnation help us understand how we eventually landed here. This "original sin" would inspire religious beliefs that defined how future societies perceived consequences and instituted the role of gender, and how governments enforced authority. It's why we say that someone who is making decisions for others is "playing God." Faith and morality served as the initial basis for how those determined what is wrong and right. Such judgment would later shape how people decided to cancel as a result. As society evolved, religious and spiritual activities began to define the terms of what it means to cancel, even if loosely. Religious texts created a framework for modern-day interpretations of morality, which laid the pathway for cancel culture. No, religion didn't invent cancel culture, but our sense of right and wrong does come from these traditions, and cancel culture gets its start there, too. In this book, I'm specifically talking about Abrahamic religions in an American context. Each religion has its own unique impact on societies around the world, and this explains why standards for what is and isn't acceptable vary from country to country. Even within religions, there are a myriad of interpretations. However, the influence of religion on cancel culture is undeniable.

WHEN IN ROME

Cancel culture could also be found in ancient Rome, which was the center of Western civilization during the early fifth century. The origins of faith-based capitalism—in the form of real estate owned by temples being relinquished to the Catholic Church—were on the rise. Christianity began to overtake the Roman Empire's own cultural expressions. Crosses were carved in pagan statues, bathhouses were converted into churches, bathing naked was outlawed, along with non-Christian rituals and songs and secular dancing. Churches were given the utmost regard, with Romans forced to lower their voices when entering the building—a practice many around the world still do as a sign of respect. Christianity was on its way to becoming the dominant force in the Western world, but many of the Roman Empire's pagan symbols, traditions, and even words were assimilated. For instance, the days of the week and the notion of welfare for the impoverished are both taken from Roman tradition.

While the course of history can appear inevitable in retrospect, there was resistance to the shift to Christianity. An Athenian philosopher, whose stance against the shift in a sixth-century text was quoted by historian Ramsay MacMullen in the 1981 book[4] *Christianity and Paganism in the Fourth to Eighth Centuries,* represents one of the rare voices of the Roman dispossessed. The

Greek philosopher described Christians as being "a race dissolved in every passion, destroyed by controlled self-indulgence, cringing and womanish in its thinking, close to cowardice, wallowing in all swinishness, debased, content with servitude in security." MacMullen was illustrating an early form of callout culture. Obviously, it was not enough to stop the rise of Christianity, but it does show how large-scale societal shifts almost always come with tension and debate.

PLYMOUTH OR BUST

Hundreds of years later, the fall of the Roman Empire was a distant memory, but the tension over religion would continue. Within the dominant religion of England in the 1600s, factions were beginning to break off. We know the travelers that sailed the *Mayflower* to America in 1620 as Pilgrims, but they were originally known as English Separatists, a radical Puritan faction that illegally broke from the Church of England. Before they left Europe on their famous voyage, they fled England for the Netherlands, where they'd go on to have religious freedom for over ten years. The Pilgrims had lived as farmers in England, but in the Dutch city of Leiden, they worked long hours for little pay in the textile industry. As well as living in extreme poverty, they faced the risk of losing their English identity.

Unable to return to England, they set their sights on the New World. Although their desire to live according to their beliefs is what is most known about the Pilgrims, the reports of financial success of New World settlers were a major factor in their decision. English companies were sponsoring crossings in order to set up outposts in America. The Pilgrims (and others) had to commit to seven years of working for these companies in exchange for the trip and a small percentage of the companies' profits.

The Pilgrims canceled their ties to the Church of England, but their immigration to America was largely driven by financial need. They took extraordinary risks by crossing the Atlantic, facing physical hardship from a land they weren't adequately prepared to live on, engaging in conflict with Indigenous people they'd assumed they could convert, and dealing with competition from other settlers, like the Puritans. The absence of opportunity, in either the Netherlands or England, meant that stepping onto the *Mayflower* was their only option. Both lack of religious freedom and economic opportunity were being rejected and canceled by the Pilgrims.

BORN IN THE U.S.A.

Although many groups—Pilgrims, Puritans, and others—were colonizing North America, they were still under some amount of control by Britain. The origins of modern American cancel culture as we know it started during the American Revolution, in the form of boycotts on British products in the colonies. After fighting the French and Indian War (1754–1763), Britain was broke and in desperate need to pay off its mounting debt. The country looked at their American colonies as the appropriate revenue generator and began taxing them on just about anything they could—namely, sugar, imported textiles, newspapers, legal documents, wines, playing cards, dice, stamps, housing arrangements, coffee, tea, and even currency itself. The Stamp Act of 1765—when the British insisted that paper products used in the colonies be manufactured in Britain and carry an embossed revenue stamp—was the straw that broke the camel's back. The British misled colonies to pay the costs of keeping English soldiers in America.

The now iconic phrase *taxation without representation* was born during this time when colonists protested that they were unfairly taxed without being allowed the right to vote for the members of Parliament who enforced such policies. America's dissatisfaction with its relationship to Britain would only grow. The biggest act of defiance during this time was the Boston Tea Party on December 16, 1773. A large group of colonial activists—led by the Sons of Liberty—disguised themselves as Native Americans in tribal garb and boarded ships full of British-owned tea that were docked at Griffin's Wharf in Boston. They smashed and dumped 340 chests of tea into the harbor.

Tossing the ninety thousand pounds of the British East India Company's valuable tea into the ocean was a protest against an unfair tea tax, but also against the unjust political control that Britain had over America.

The Boston Tea Party became one of the most successful boycotts of the American Revolution and inspired colonists to stop buying British goods when it was possible. There were threats of violence wielded at the tax inspectors who imposed these harsh policies. As a result, many of those tax inspectors were forced to resign, and Britain consequently repealed the Stamp Act in 1766. This early example of cancel culture in the name of independence, free speech, and liberty makes it more ironic that Republicans, who consider themselves reverent patriots, are some of the biggest opponents of cancel culture. The very foundation of their constitutional fundamentalism was built off the backs of protesters who dumped tea into the harbor and called for boycotts of government policies that oppressed them.

Conservatives who argue that cancel culture is "un-American" ignore history altogether. It is literally the basis of our governing documents. The Constitution wouldn't exist without the defiance of the colonists who resisted British tyranny. The American Revolution was the result of adamant protest against an oppressive power. They fought back against the British, whom they felt were infringing upon their geopolitical sovereignty. While their own white supremacy had infringed upon the livelihoods of enslaved Africans and Indigenous Americans, they were also terrorized by the forces of King George III. In this case, two things were true at the same time: Colonists were canceling British oppressive rule, while simultaneously denying the freedoms and liberties of Black and Indigenous American people. It would take an entire Civil War, the Reconstruction era, and the civil rights movement before notable changes from the descendants of these colonists would help them understand such legislative hypocrisy. The lack of reparations for either group speaks volumes to how this country really feels about how it treated Black and Indigenous Americans.

ALL MEN ARE CREATED EQUAL

The abolition movement of the nineteenth century was a pivotal moment in how cancel culture evolved into the social justice movement we are currently witnessing today. In the 1800s, American abolitionists wanted to end slavery in a country that had a Declaration of Independence that said, "All men are created equal." Up until that moment in American history, cancel culture had been used to address geopolitical independence. Abolitionists used cancel culture for social justice. After witnessing British abolitionists succeed in ending slavery in the 1830s, many felt it was time for America to catch up to the country they once deemed oppressive and tyrannical.

American abolitionists were ready to bring that kind of energy and action to a government that had prided itself on being more democratic than Great Britain. Abolitionists used the free press to question America's morals and values as slaveholders. Colonists had previously written books and op-eds in their local newspapers that questioned British rule, but American abolitionists expressed themselves even further through organizing. Before future generations would voice their opinions on social media, abolitionists utilized free speech in similar ways prior to cancel culture being modernized.

Unlike the white protesters before them who could openly demonstrate against the British, Black Americans did not have the same freedom, whether they were free or enslaved. Black abolitionists, such as Frederick Douglass and Sojourner Truth, used the power of the pen and speech to call for the end of slavery. Douglass's 1845 memoir,[5] *A Narrative of the Life of Frederick Douglass, an American Slave,* and the founding of his antislavery newspaper *The North Star* in 1847 gave America the rare perspective of a freed Black man who knew too well the harms of being enslaved. Truth's 1851 speech[6] "Ain't I a Woman" put a mirror up to the limited scope of American womanhood at a time that denied Black women rights and freedoms. The strategic devices of written and spoken word used by these Black abolitionists would inspire future generations of activists, including those within hip-hop and poetry spaces. Martin Luther King

Jr.'s 1963[7] "I Have a Dream" is one of the best-known speeches in history, and he and his message helped galvanize the civil rights movement of the 1960s. In 2020, the late Freedom Rider and American congressman John Lewis gave a speech on the Edmund Pettus Bridge, in Selma, Alabama, to commemorate the tragic events of 1965's Bloody Sunday. He encouraged young people[8] to get into "good trouble, necessary trouble," a phrase that was instantly taken up by many contemporary activists. Like current calls to defund the police, a movement aimed at divesting in policing by reinvesting in alternative community measures (and wildly oversimplified by the mainstream media as being anarchist), pro-abolition at the time was considered a radical concept. American legislators of the 1800s couldn't fathom the idea of Black people being granted the same rights as they had. It would even take ninety-nine years after the 1865 ratification of the Thirteenth Amendment abolishing slavery before Black people were granted legislative equality via the Civil Rights Act of 1964. Imagine that: Calls to cancel slavery in America were considered problematic and divisive. Let this serve as a litmus test of how current calls for progress might be ahead of their time.

The move to cancel slavery was so politically polarizing that it led to the Civil War—an epic fight between Northern and Southern states. Southern states relied on slave labor for their economic survival and were willing to cancel the America we know today to hold on to their ability to enslave other human beings. The formulation of the Confederacy was cancel culture in its purest—albeit twisted—sense. Southern states, just like their colonist ancestors, felt that their liberties were being infringed upon. As a result, they decided to break away from the union to protest what they perceived to be a violation of their "state's rights" according to the Constitution. As we'll see throughout the book, the effort to maintain the status quo is a hallmark of conservative cancel culture. The rebellion would lead to the deadliest war on American soil and a Reconstruction era that pledged to prevent such extreme, polarizing political division in the future. While our current political climate is deeply fractured between liberals and conservatives, there has yet to be another geographical war among American states like what happened between 1861 and 1865.

What occurred in the latter half of the nineteenth century would shape cancel culture as we know it. Abolitionists brought cancel culture from a fight over national sovereignty to the ability for all people to have personal sovereignty. Whereas the American Revolution was a bold statement for democracy against an authoritarian government, and certain unalienable rights for some, abolitionists were calling for freedom based on human rights for all. For the first time in American history, there was a movement calling for human rights. Rather than simply demanding "give me liberty or give me death," questions like "What to the slave is the Fourth of July?"

challenged morality and institutions simultaneously. It was in this era of cancel culture where the *what* became more about the *who*—humanity was at the forefront of the movement, rather than power via property.

TWENTIETH-CENTURY AMERICA

By the early twentieth century, the white descendants of American colonists controlled a soon-to-be global superpower that put them in the front seat of wealth and privilege. White men were the ruling class, with Black and Brown people, women, LGBTQIA people, non-Christians, and immigrants existing as marginalized people. The distinctions between straight white men and the rest of American society inspired activist groups to form following the Reconstruction era. In 1909, an interracial group of progressives formed the National Association for the Advancement of Colored People (NAACP). Incorporating the early teachings of abolitionists, this organization was focused on civil rights at a time when segregation was continuing to reveal the hypocrisy of "separate but equal" policies.

One of the first major boycotts by the NAACP came in 1915, when they called for theaters to stop playing the controversial film *The Birth of a Nation*. The movie positively portrayed the Ku Klux Klan, while perpetuating racist, harmful stereotypes of Black people. The campaign to cancel the film wasn't successful, and the film was shown all over America (with some minor edits in certain cities), but the action heralded a new expression of cancel culture. The NAACP's boycott was pivotal because it wasn't simply about a particular law or direct physical harm that an institution had caused. This was about the *implication* of the film. Unlike British tea and slave-produced sugar, *The Birth of a Nation* was being called out by the NAACP for how it made a community *feel* and how it would influence the way the world perceived Black people. Whereas previous boycotts, like the boycott against slave-produced sugar, were rooted in economics, this was rooted in something based largely on moral judgment and the impact on human dignity. This action helped revolutionize how consumers would later apply emotional appeals to cancel culture. We saw this kind of action play out in 2021 with calls for Netflix to remove Dave Chappelle's comedy special because of his hateful and harmful jokes about transgender people.

In 1917, the NAACP would again try to make racial progress and got over ten thousand people to participate in a silent protest in New York City against the continual lynching of Black people. Despite hosting one of the first mass demonstrations against racial violence in America, the organization still failed to get a federal anti-lynching law passed as a result. This wasn't because NAACP leaders lacked the tenacity and passion to demand change— they were just living in a society that felt that legislatively canceling lynching, a grotesque violation of humanity, wasn't necessary.

A successful case of cancel culture occurred shortly after this, in the 1920s, when the Anti-Defamation League (ADL) organized a boycott and sued automobile mogul[9] Henry Ford for libel after he published several anti-Semitic articles in *The Dearborn Independent,* a newspaper he owned. Founded in 1913, the ADL is a Jewish-led organization that has a storied reputation for going after public figures, companies, and institutions they deem anti-Semitic. Their attempt to cancel *The Dearborn Independent* must have seemed outrageously ambitious, given the power of the Ford Motor Company and its CEO, but it worked. The lawsuit, along with many Jewish Americans and their Christian allies calling on people to stop purchasing cars from the company, forced Ford to shut down the polarizing publication in 1927.

1930s INDIA

As these issues grew in America, the 1930s would also see calls for equality and justice in India through the civil disobedience of Mahatma Gandhi. When Great Britain ruled India via the British East India Company, they enforced a salt tax—which penalized Indians for buying their native salt instead of purchasing it from the British. The salt tax had long suppressed the economic freedom of Indians. Gandhi, an activist who spent twenty years in South Africa, returned with a bolder vision to confront the injustice his people faced.

Gandhi encouraged the approach[10] of satyagraha, also known as mass civil disobedience, and rallied the Salt March. In 1930, he mobilized thousands of Indians to go to the Arabian Sea coast and make salt from the seawater themselves. Thousands of Indians across the region participated, sparking the British authorities to arrest over sixty thousand people. This activism exposed how excessive and bullish the British were in the international press, which promoted immediate global outrage. Coordinated civil disobedience—the act of nonviolent activism that would prompt arrests—is quintessential to the modern-day protests we have now come to expect in the U.S. and across the globe. Making international headlines that revealed injustice was the "going viral" of that time. These acts of mass civil disobedience demanded public attention because their ambitious execution couldn't be ignored. The public shaming of government officials and institutions who violated the rights of others was elevated in these deliberate acts of cancel culture. *Time* magazine named Gandhi "Man of the Year" and compared the Salt March to the Boston Tea Party. The success of the Salt March inspired other similar acts by Gandhi and forced the British government to relinquish its firm control of India. Years later, civil rights icon Dr. Martin Luther King Jr. would apply

Gandhi's radical techniques to his own approach of canceling racial segregation in America.

WHO IS CANCELING WHOM?

Until the latter half of the twentieth century, American society was obsessed with a certain level of conformity that was driven by Judeo-Christian values and socially acceptable racism. A woman's role was in the home raising children. Church was integral to the American family. Homosexuality was considered a perversion, along with premarital sex and birth control. Patriotism was a religion within itself, as the nation's flag was—and still is—often greeted with the Pledge of Allegiance that includes "one nation under God." With the end of World War II, white Americans felt like they were on top of the world. The axis of power tilted in America's favor; we were a superpower promoting democracy as the new standard of governance.

Such growing patriotism on the part of white Americans disguised itself as a social justice movement, but the cancel culture involved was the complete opposite. While the NAACP and ADL continued to focus on combating discrimination and bigotry, conservative white Americans were pursuing their own cause. There's no better example of the early rise of conservative cancel culture than McCarthyism in the 1950s. The infamous term is named after

U.S. senator Joseph McCarthy of Wisconsin, the Republican politician who pushed the Second Red Scare at a time when American fear of Communism was at an all-time high. As America emerged as a global leader after World War II, there was an ongoing fear that anarchism could potentially upend its status. Communism, which was embraced by our Soviet Union rivals at the time, was and continues to be a scarlet letter for anyone in American politics. The United States was growing fearful and weary of being involved in the Korean War while observing the constant presence of Communism in Eastern Europe and China. McCarthy capitalized on this growing sentiment and built his political career on the exposure and destruction of Communism in America.

"One thing to remember in discussing the Communists in our government is that we are not dealing with spies who get thirty pieces of silver to steal the blueprints of a new weapon," McCarthy said in a 1950 speech,[11] when he claimed that fifty-seven Communists had infiltrated the State Department. "We are dealing with a far more sinister type of activity because it permits the enemy to guide and shape our policy."

McCarthy became the chair of the Committee on Government Operations of the Senate and of its permanent subcommittee on investigations. For the next two years, he wasted precious resources and taxpayer money accusing various individuals and institutions of Communist affiliations. Everyone from famed director Orson Welles to lauded poet Langston Hughes was interrogated by members of McCarthy's infamous House Un-American Activities Committee (HUAC). There they were asked the notorious question: "Are you now or have you ever been a member of the Communist Party?"

Despite his aggressive pursuit to rid America of Communism, McCarthy failed to make a serious case against anyone he accused. However, his over-the-top accusations on live television were enough to publicly shame and damage the reputations of those he called to the carpet. He went so far as to threaten Democratic senator Lester Hunt, who was an outspoken opponent of McCarthy's anti-Communist campaign. After Hunt's son was arrested for soliciting sex from an undercover male police officer pretending to be gay, McCarthy said he'd prosecute the young man and publicize the events if Hunt ran for reelection. Hunt committed suicide soon after.

In 1954, the fall came swiftly for McCarthyism after an epic thirty-six days of televised investigative hearings led by the soon-to-be-disgraced senator. The entire nation was able to watch the media circus McCarthy had created. But his humbling moment was made memorable in the form of a rhetorical question posed by Joseph Welch, an attorney McCarthy had interrogated and accused of hiring a man who once belonged to a Communist-front group.

"Have you no sense of decency, sir, at long last?" Welch sternly asked McCarthy. "Have you left no sense of decency?"

Soon public opinion turned on McCarthy and his investigations. Legendary journalist Edward R. Murrow undermined McCarthy's credibility through a television editorial that would reshape what accountability in the media would look like. This helped lead the charge to McCarthy being censured—a rare action taken by the Senate—for what they found to be conduct unbecoming of a senator. He died shortly after in 1957 as a disgraced politician whose legacy of attempting to cancel so many renowned creatives, activists, and innocent people had backfired, ending in his own cancellation.

McCarthy's persecution of innocent Americans would later be deemed a witch hunt. The origin of that term harkens back to the Salem witch trials of the 1600s.[12] What started with a group of girls accusing several women of casting spells, ended in a mass hysteria that saw hundreds accused and many executed. It's ironic that many conservatives today claim that cancel culture is a witch hunt against their own civil liberties. The staff of the Salem Witch Museum came up with an equation for isolating what makes a witch hunt: fear + trigger = scapegoat. In the case of Salem, there was a fear of the supernatural and of women's supposed inborn evil, the trigger was some teenage girls believing they witnessed unnatural behavior, and the scapegoats were the nineteen women who were hanged. While it's true that a witch hunt is an unfair persecution, a person justifiably being held to account can hardly claim they're the victim of a witch hunt.

COUNTERCULTURE

The cancellation of McCarthyism was a harbinger of the countercultural movement. The 1950s was a key decade in the trajectory of cancel culture in America. At that point, dominant society insisted on a conservative way of life that was built around Judeo-Christian moral principles of decency and respectability. The first half of the twentieth century enforced social conformity in a democracy that claimed it promoted life, liberty, and the pursuit of happiness. But these norms were as hypocritical as they'd been a century before (and continue to be to this day, in some cases). How can a country that calls itself the beacon of free speech and democracy restrict the freedoms of the very citizens it considers free? In the nineteenth century, Black people were still considered enslaved property and only three-fifths of a person. Even after slavery was abolished, Jim Crow laws insisted that Black Americans were "equal but separate" and required segregation of everything from schools to seats on buses. Greater racial diversity in film, music, and media in the 1950s caused a younger generation of white people to begin questioning their parents' attitudes. While not completely detached from their racist and sexist upbringings, boomers were more progressive than their ultraconservative parents. Their taste for rock and roll music, an embracement of Black images in cinema, and the departure from some of the more patriarchal standards of family life (the seeds for which were sown during World War II when women joined the workforce in great numbers) helped lay the groundwork for how the counterculture movement would take off.

The counterculture movement helped redefine the way we think about cancel culture as a cultural war that is shaped by identity politics. Identity politics describes an affiliation that is based on race, gender, sexuality, or other identifying factors—rather than simply a party affiliation. Centuries of martyrdom, boycotts, abolition, and protests would reveal that the new fight was beyond political stances and economics, encompassing who we are and what kind of society we want to live in. The countercultural movement empowered marginalized communities, such as people of color, women, and LGBTQIA individuals, to act and boycott institutions and individuals who impeded or infringed upon their civil liberties. Coalitions were formed, meaning that people were aware of and supportive of causes even if they weren't personally affected.

Mass media and the coverage of various social justice movements allowed many more people to become aware of identity politics in a new way. A more diverse media landscape, subtle racial integration, and the increased political polarization of society sped up the way

Americans canceled each other. Every night offered an opportunity for Americans to catch up on events happening at home and around the world. For example, the 1960 televised presidential debate, featuring a split screen with then senator John F. Kennedy and Vice President Richard Nixon, changed forever how Americans would consume politics. The placement of a pale, sickly, underweight, and tired Nixon next to a more energized, tanned Kennedy influenced public opinion about the former's performance. Seventy million people watched that first debate, and it became symbolic of how America viewed the world they were living in. In a pre-televised era, an older patriarch might have been the de facto winner. Instead, the broadcasted youthquake of the 1960s was beginning to rumble. Kennedy projected energy and confidence, while Nixon was sweating. The contrast left many Americans feeling like Nixon was untrustworthy. At forty-three years old, Kennedy would go on to defeat Nixon and become the youngest person to become a U.S. president by election.

AND NOW

The current iteration of cancel culture takes the form of multiple individualistic actions that speak to collective advancement against some form of oppression, whether perceived or real. In other words, many agitated people acting independently—yet in concert with others—either through in-person protests or on platforms such as social media can create a demand for change. The protesters outside of an Amazon warehouse demanding better workers' rights are not simply fighting for themselves, they are also fighting against the way unbridled capitalism hurts people everywhere. When former NFL football player Colin Kaepernick knelt during the national anthem on September 1, 2016, his act of defiance against patriotism was in solidarity with Black Lives Matter protests against extrajudicial murders of Black and Brown people by the police. In both situations, whether calling for the cancellation of Amazon's current workplace policies or excessive police force—those who choose to act are doing so for a cause that is bigger than only their individual gripe. As we'll see throughout the book, this is characteristic of progressive cancel culture. There's an inclusive quality to it, and the motto could be "What's bad for some is bad for us all."

Modern cancel culture is essentially a boycott—a protest that seeks to end something or someone based on a harm that was caused. In this dynamic, interpretations and perceptions of harm belong to the offended, with the decision to cancel being levied by that person and their supporters. The terms and levels of cancellation can vary based on the magnitude of the situation. In 2021, when Georgia legislators passed regressive voter laws, activists succeeded in calling on companies and organizations to stop doing business with the state to force them to reconsider. In 2017, Black activists Kenyette Tisha Barnes and Oronike Odeleye created the #MuteRKelly movement that called for the conviction of the disgraced R&B singer and for his fans to financially divest from him after he faced multiple charges of sexual abuse. Over the years, LGBTQIA groups have called on people to not buy from certain companies, such as Chick-fil-A, the Salvation Army, and Urban Outfitters, because of their anti-LGBTQIA stances or investments. In all these situations, a direct call to action was issued, but each received a different level of engagement based on the immediate severity of the situation and institution.

Let's go back to Georgia. Georgia lawmakers, with their institutional power, deserved aggressive consequences for imposing sweeping new restrictions on voting access. This is starkly different from tweeting at consumers to not buy a chicken sandwich from a fast-food spot that is closed on Sundays. And part of that is because of the relationship of the players involved. The actions of Chick-fil-A are a drop in the bucket of the overall anti-LGBTQIA movement. Georgia lawmakers, on the other hand, by passing statewide laws and emboldening other conservative states to do the same, required a sharper form of cancellation. Pro-democracy activists were able to use both on-the-ground methods and all forms of media to spread their message.

It's popular to claim that social media is responsible for cancel culture. That's putting the cart before the horse. Before there were touch screens, there were keyboards.

Before that, there were typewriters, and before that, there were quills and ink. Before Twitter, there were blogs, newspapers, and petitions. Social media amplified cancel culture, but it did not invent it.

"The history of cancel culture has evolved alongside the way we communicate," says Dr. Crystal M. Edwards, an education activist and researcher. "The advancements in *how* we communicate directly reflects on how we 'cancel' those things within our culture that are deemed unacceptable. During the Civil War, you waited for a person to ride a horse to deliver a letter. During Jim Crow, you waited on the postman to deliver on your delivery day. During the civil rights era, you waited for daily mail, phone calls, telegrams. Iran Contra, it was Federal Express. O. J. Simpson trial, it was an email. As communication modes evolved, so did our cancel culture methods."

"There have always been various methods of public shaming and holding people accountable in respective communities," says William Ketchum III, a senior culture editor and journalist at Mic, an online culture magazine. "The major difference now is that with social media and the internet, it's easier to be shamed by communities you're barely even a part of." Meaning that a person can get involved in the cancellation of someone across the country, if it's an issue they feel strongly about. "That shame has both more permanence and more temporality at the same time. We live in an era where people's differing experiences are receiving more recognition, so that there are more reasons for people to be shamed in the first place for not recognizing those issues." There are fewer and fewer excuses for people to claim ignorance about the life experiences of others. If there's a will to understand someone else's experience, there is certainly a way.

Understanding the ways that cancel culture can be used to advance certain causes doesn't make the trajectory to justice any simpler. Nothing moves in a straight line. The same nation that instituted a federal holiday in honor of Martin Luther King Jr. went on to elect a racist president who strove to destroy the very fabric of equality and nonviolence MLK once preached. The same nation that once considered interracial marriage a crime later elected as president a man born of a Black father and a white mother, twice.

Whether it's being used to maintain the status quo or move the culture forward, cancel culture is as American as apple pie and as essential to our democracy as the Constitution it helped inspire. These actions not only speak to the identity of America but have shaped how the world has operated since the very beginning. There is nothing new under the sun, and cancel culture is a prime example.

WHEN CANCELING WAS
THE ONLY OPTION

Cancel culture is not the spontaneous whim it's often
characterized as but can serve as an intentional, final
move when all hope is lost for the marginalized.

On March 24, 2018, more than 1.2 million people across America protested to cancel our nation's pervasive gun culture. Following the tragic
school shooting at Marjory Stoneman Douglas High
School in Parkland, Florida, earlier that year, Cameron
Kasky and his classmates quickly organized an event to
galvanize public opinion around gun violence. The protest
was led by progressive Gen Zers who were fed up with
the ongoing gun violence that had taken the lives of their
family and friends, and essentially, their future. The target was the National Rifle Association, the controversial
group that lobbies for gun ownership and reduced regu-
lations. This protest was just as much about calling for
the NRA's demise as it was about calling on legislators to
finally act. As one of the largest protests in American history, the March for Our Lives was a message,[1] made loud
and clear, that cancel culture was the only plausible option

left after years of government resistance to sensible gun control legislation. It had become accepted wisdom that going up against the NRA was a fool's errand, and that any politician or activist group who tried it would lose. These kids were telling the world they had nothing left to lose.

"To the leaders, skeptics, and cynics who told us to sit down and stay silent: Wait your turn," Kasky said to the crowd during the Washington, D.C., rally. "Welcome to the revolution."

"To all the politicians out there, if you take money from the NRA, you have chosen death," Alex Wind, a junior at Stoneman Douglas at the time, told the audience. "If you have not expressed to your constituents a public stance on this issue, you have chosen death. If you do not stand with us by saying we need to pass common-sense gun legislation, you have chosen death. And none of the millions of people marching in this country today will stop until they see those against us out of office, because we choose life."

The impact of the March for Our Lives was pivotal in putting the national gun violence debate back in the public eye. After previous mass shootings, including the tragic Pulse nightclub incident in 2016 and Sandy Hook Elementary School attack in 2012, the redundant "thoughts and prayers to the victims" statement would go out from liberal and conservative politicians alike, with very little follow-up. Sure, there would often be a high-profile can-

dlelight vigil or temporary public awareness campaigns—
such as when a group of liberal celebrities got together
to push the Demand a Plan on gun control public service announcement in December 2012 following Sandy
Hook. But a collective movement to overhaul gun culture
in America had yet to be carried out on a massive scale.

The March for Our Lives reflected pent-up frustration
from a new generation who was fed up with the apathy of
their elders. To them, there was a lot of talk and no walk
when it came to demanding universal background checks
on gun sales and a ban on assault rifles. They wanted
guns gone or at least harder to obtain. They didn't care if
their demands made them appear to be radical or polarizing, for the cost of complicity with the status quo had
proven to be death.

What separated this movement from previous anti-
gun groups was the reaction to it. While many lauded
these young people for speaking out, right-wing media,
the NRA, and its proxies chose to go on the offensive.
In a disappointing move, the Right launched attacks on
the teen leaders of the March for Our Lives movement.
Fox News anchor Tucker Carlson whined that Emma
González, David Hogg, Sam Fuentes, and the rest were
just "self-righteous kids screaming at you on TV." Meghan
McCain spouted that Hogg's use of the f-word wasn't
productive. Republican Maine State House candidate
Leslie Gibson said González was a "skinhead lesbian"
who did nothing to impress her. Suffice to say, it was a

bad look. Unless, of course, the Right was hoping to help crystallize the David-and-Goliath image by criticizing kids for not wanting to be shot at school.

Like many other people throughout history, the youth behind the March for Our Lives were using cancel culture because it was their only option. Most of them were too young to vote or run for office—two more traditional ways of making change. They lacked a traditional kind of power. With the help of social media, they mobilized the public and galvanized resources to call for stronger gun control. David Hogg posted an NRA-style ad on Twitter, asking, "What if our politicians weren't the bitch of the NRA?" They held protests, organized school walkouts, created petitions, demanded legislative change to end assault weapons being sold commercially. In the end, they succeeded in making gun control a top policy issue that has yet to leave the public's consciousness. Cancel culture was something that no one could stop them from enacting.

This last-chance quality can be seen in cancel culture throughout history. In 1964, during a speech with Malcom X at a rally at the Williams Institutional CME Church in Harlem, civil rights icon Fannie Lou Hamer spoke these famous words: "All my life I've been sick and tired. Now I'm sick and tired of being sick and tired."

Hamer, who was running for the U.S. Senate in the Jim Crow South, was a leader of the Mississippi Freedom Democratic Party, an organization that was calling out discriminatory voting practices at the time. The state of Mississippi made it extremely difficult for Black people to vote. Hamer herself had to write the associated literacy test three times before passing it and being allowed to vote. There is no doubt that Hamer knew she was going to lose her election, given the racist voter suppression she faced, making her determination to call out the injustice even nobler. Her campaign was an indictment of American racism and how it oppressed its most diverse citizens.

Calls for the cancellation of Jim Crow laws were motivated by a group of people who were sick and tired of being sick and tired of the rampant white supremacy they experienced. Given how the Black vote was suppressed, cancel culture became their only available option. Although she didn't win a seat in the Senate, Hamer continued her activism by giving speeches at universities and colleges, as well as working on Martin Luther King Jr.'s Poor People's Campaign and launching the Freedom Farm Cooperative. In the end, Hamer's activism did more than she probably could have ever done in office, advancing the voting rights of Black and Brown Southerners and leading efforts to help fracture the legislative white supremacy of Mississippi at a time when it felt impossible. In 1964, Jim Crow laws were overturned by the Civil Rights Act and in 1965 by the Voting Rights Act. The breakthroughs of Shirley Chisholm, Hillary Clinton, Kamala Harris, Stacey Abrams, and many others would have not been achievable without the radical racial and gender inclusions Hamer politically fought for with her acts of civil disobedience. The successes we now hold in such high regard today came, at least in part, from a cancel culture that was pursued by someone who'd had enough with the status quo, even though she began from a place of very little power.

Some systems of power are nearly impossible to change from within. Hollywood, it turns out, is one of those systems. The performers who came out in numbers to share their experiences of being sexually harassed and abused during the rise of the #MeToo movement (which, of course, grew to encompass many industries and work-places outside of Hollywood as well) did so because they had suffered silently for years. Maybe they'd tried to qui-etly manage the situation. Maybe they'd even warned each other about dangerous bosses. Many of those survivors, including actresses such as Lupita Nyong'o and Salma Hayek, did not originally seek to cancel the once-illustrious Hollywood career of convicted sex offender Harvey Wein-stein. However, cancellation eventually became a necessity when there were no other options available. Their careers, safety, and livelihoods depended on it.

In a December 2017 op-ed for *The New York Times*,[2] Hayek wrote extensively about the sexual harassment she experienced from Weinstein while producing the 2002 film *Frida*—ranging from requesting that she take a shower with him to asking if he could perform oral sex on her—and the retaliation that would come from rejecting him. "I don't think he hated anything more than the word 'no,'" Hayek wrote. "And with every refusal came Harvey's Machiavellian rage."

In the op-ed, Hayek recalls that Weinstein treated her differently "when he was finally convinced that I was not going to earn the movie the way he had expected" and tried to give the role she had perfected for years to another actress as a form of punishment. After she threatened to sue, Weinstein gave Hayek what she described as "a list of impossible tasks," which involved raising $10 million for the film, securing a critically acclaimed director, and securing other A-list costars. After she achieved these lofty, nearly impossible goals—Hayek was then beholden to Weinstein, who "was not only rejected but also about to do a movie he did not want to do." She would then endure multiple instances of animosity, emotional abuse, and career setbacks because of her initial refusal to have sex with Weinstein. It would not be until she broke her silence during the #MeToo movement that her career struggles were explained. Many other actresses would come forward with stories of enduring Weinstein's horrific behavior. And no wonder they were afraid to talk about it; Weinstein had been able to ruin the careers of many actresses just for rejecting him. What would he do if they told the truth about their encounters with him? Weinstein's power in Hollywood was supersized, and he was known for wielding his power ruthlessly. Though it seems baffling, such abuses were, and still are, an open secret in Hollywood, and no one seems to care about the victims until the industry is forced to acknowledge it.

The cancellation of Weinstein was long, drawn out, and painful for the victims (on top of the pain they had already endured). Yet it became the only solution for women like Hayek who had no other options and little else to lose. As the students at Marjory Stoneman Douglas High School, Hamer, and Hayek all learned, cancel culture is not something to act on lightly. It must be rooted in addressing forces that represent a threat to a person or group's full existence. A person's right to life, freedom, and dignity must be threatened to merit the extremeness of cancellation. And when it comes to extremes, both the potential effects of cancellation and the effort/risk-taking required to cancel must be fully considered.

White supremacy merits cancellation because it seeks to erode diversity, equity, and inclusion of non-white people. Gun violence merits cancellation because it is a matter of life and death. Sexual assault merits cancellation. But if someone on social media tells the world not to eat chocolate cake because they don't like the taste, that isn't cancel culture. Chocolate cake cannot threaten anyone's life and liberty. Now, if the company making the chocolate cake is supporting anti-LGBTQIA causes—said chocolate cake would be a symbol of bigotry and could be canceled. Remember, tea wasn't canceled by the Sons of Liberty because of its taste but because it was overtaxed by the oppressive British monarchy at the time. Personal tastes don't dictate cancel culture. Contrary to the opinions of mainstream pundits and critics, everyone and everything isn't being canceled.

"When we talk about canceling someone, in many cases we are talking about an abuse of power. Someone commits an act so heinous, violent, or unethical, that those calling them out or demanding that they either relinquish the power that they abused or that their power be taken away—whether it's their high-powered job or role in government," says Daniela Capistrano, a queer nonbinary activist and founder/CEO of DCAP MEDIA. "On the interpersonal level, often 'canceling' someone is an act of self-preservation. The person canceling the other person has decided that they aren't going to spend any more time trying to educate the offender—to help them see the light. They are simply going to publicly disclose the harm they experienced at the hands of this person and then cut them out of their life—with the idea that perhaps others will follow suit." Capistrano makes a good point in that you can't always control the outcome of cancel culture. You can speak your truth and hope that encourages other people to join you, but you may find it necessary to go ahead and make your statement without knowing if they will.

Cancel culture is political, deliberate, and conscious. It's not a matter of taste, a difference of opinion, or simply a publicity stunt. Whether someone is ultraconservative or Far Left, the decision-making behind canceling something is based in one's fundamental desire to survive and feel safe. Individual interpretations on what's right and wrong will forever be debated—but that's not what makes something cancel culture or not.

For example, when Jack Phillips, a Colorado baker, refused[3] to create a custom wedding cake for a same-sex couple in 2012, he was participating in his own form of cancel culture because he believed that doing such a task infringed on his religious beliefs, which can be an extreme matter of heaven or hell to some. The Colorado Court of Appeals rejected Phillips's claim and said his actions defied Colorado's anti-discrimination laws. The Supreme Court, however, would later rule in 2018 that the state exhibited "religious hostility" against him. Whether society agreed with the measures taken by Phillips or not, his rationale for why he decided to cancel serving a same-sex couple a wedding cake perfectly fits what cancel culture truly is. For him, doing so was forcing him to compromise his religious beliefs beyond the threshold of standard decency. Had Phillips refused to serve them a non-wedding cake simply for being gay— that would have been discriminatory and based on their identity alone. But the Supreme Court argued that forcing Phillips to make a cake for a same-sex wedding in particular—a ceremonial practice that his faith defines as being between a man and a woman—was hostile to his religious beliefs. Similarly, a Black baker could refuse to make a cake that had white supremacy rhetoric written on it because the message threatened their way of life. In other words, cancel culture is a tactic—not just a stance taken solely by conservatives or progressives.

Since the beginning of time, opinions have been shared, whether they were informed or not. These kinds of critiques shape the way we view the world around us. Many believe cancel culture is just about criticizing something you don't like, as if it's simply individuals venting in public for a reaction. Critics aren't in the business of canceling things; they simply give their perspective on how they feel we should consume something. This isn't cancel culture. Professional critics aren't responsible for dictating and/or mobilizing legislative/social change; they simply give you a thorough take that offers you the agency to decide for yourself. The way the internet, and largely social media, has blurred the lines between general criticism and cancel culture has been a disservice to the public.

When celebrities complain about a bad review, they can't blame it on cancel culture. When people took to social media to express their disdain for the 2020 film *Wonder Woman 1984,* the movie didn't pose a threat to anyone's humanity. Sure, some felt the movie wasted a precious two hours they couldn't ever get back—but that was due to massive plot holes and lukewarm acting. As we discussed in the previous chapter, when the NAACP boycotted the 1915 silent film *The Birth of a Nation,* it was a form of cancel culture because the movie was attempting to demoralize and promote violence toward

Black people. The film was being canceled by Black activists and allies because it was cinematic white supremacy, not just a movie that had lackluster cinematography and writing. There were similar complaints of racism surrounding classic films[4] such as *Gone with the Wind* and *Breakfast at Tiffany's,* which also faced calls for the public not to watch them. When debates around personal opinions and cancel culture are treated as being one and the same, we lose the ability to recognize matters that require direct action.

Confusion over what cancel culture is has often been used to reduce its actual efficacy, with critics making it a new, problematic trend rather than a reflection of the fierce determination to demand something better. The fact that many people persist in acting on cancel culture in the face of cultural confusion over its meaning only underlines its necessity. On the other hand, many have taken part in cancel culture more often than they realize, for an imperfect society demands it. When you choose to go green or vegan, you are a part of the cancellation of fossil fuels and livestock farming to protect the environment. When you promote anti-smoking policies in buildings, you are a part of canceling cigarettes because you believe they cause harm. All these examples seek to promote actions that individuals believe will make the world a better place. The bold declarations and ways these ideals are carried out makes it cancel culture. For example, one can believe that climate change is real and that something should be done—but unless you actively decide to reduce usage of products that waste precious resources, you're not part of cancel culture.

Cancel culture takes place when the ability to compromise or negotiate expires. It's when the cup has runneth over and there's no place to go but the streets. It's when the backdoor meetings, prior warnings, and other proactive attempts to find a resolution cease to exist. Cancel culture isn't the first option but the last resort—one that should never be taken lightly. Which is why arguments over-projecting cancel culture as being massively widespread are patently false. Opinions and complaints on social media don't automatically equate to cancel culture, because many don't seek to address something that is harming their way of life. Philadelphia 76ers fans were furious over the way NBA All-Star Ben Simmons handled his eventual trade to the Brooklyn Nets. While he was still on the Sixers bench, they chanted, "Fuck Ben Simmons!" Was he canceled? Have a look at his $33-million-a-year salary with the Nets, if you're curious. Grievances must be more elevated than that for them to be considered cancel culture.

The other problem with dismissing cancel culture as merely a method for those upset about something is that this position fails to take into consideration the effort and risk-taking required to cancel. It's not easy to protest continuously. It could not have been easy for those Parkland teens to live through the trauma of a school shooting, only to be attacked in the media for their protest. It must have been exhausting for Fannie Lou Hamer to have to fight—over and over and over—for her ability to simply vote in the country where she was a citizen. In calling out Harvey Weinstein, Salma Hayek experienced a loss of time and money, faced public embarrassment, and risked being blackballed in her industry. Just because cancel culture is frequently the only option for oppressed individuals or groups doesn't mean that it is easy or that it comes without cost—especially given that they aren't just seeking attention.

These scenarios clarify the weight and intentionality behind cancel culture and explain why it isn't as passive, petty, or vapid as presumed by critics. While some may try to suggest that practically anything *can* be canceled, the fact of the matter is that most things *aren't and won't be*. Despite how prevalent sexism and racism are in society, they haven't been completely terminated. This is because there are opposing forces that are actively working to keep these systems in place. If it were so easy to wipe out the reputation or standing of a person or a movement, wouldn't all racists and sexists be canceled by now?

It's often the case that those who claim to have been canceled, or seem to have been canceled, are far from it. During a conversation between comedian Conan O'Brien and actor Sean Penn[5] on O'Brien's podcast, *Conan O'Brien Needs a Friend,* in July 2021, the two bemoaned the terrible results of cancel culture. "When we're destroying careers like that, what are we really achieving?" Penn asked, referring to Alexi McCammond, the young political reporter who was ousted[6] as editor in chief of *Teen Vogue* in March 2021 after a series of anti-Asian and homophobic tweets she had posted as a teenager resurfaced. Enough was enough—these two men felt like cancel culture was doing more harm than good to people who'd been shortsighted in their pasts. Woe to the person who simply made a poor choice and now must be doomed for eternity for it.

The truth is, McCammond was seventeen when she tweeted about a "stupid Asian" teaching assistant and hoping she wouldn't wake up with "swollen Asian eyes," among other things. She wasn't an adult, but she wasn't a child either—she was a high school senior. After being pressured by both *Teen Vogue* staffers and advertisers, Condé Nast made the decision to not go ahead with McCammond's hire. She ended up going back to her job as a political reporter at Axios. There's no doubt that it was likely a very unpleasant experience to be so publicly dumped from a high-profile gig—but McCammond's career was not destroyed or canceled.

"Being held accountable for your words, deeds, and actions used to be something that was only possible on a micro, person-to-person, community level," says digital strategist and organizer Leslie Mac. "As our world has gotten smaller via technology, the ability to hold someone accountable has only grown larger." In the case of McCammond, she was held accountable both from people who would be working with her—the staff of *Teen Vogue*—and organizations out in the world who had heard about her behavior—advertisers. Mac goes on, "It is a good thing that people in NYC know the harm someone caused in Houston—this is how we stop people from continuing their bad behavior."

"As a survivor and abolitionist, I have realized that while I do not want harm doers to be incarcerated, and we should instead engage in transformative justice, I do believe that 'cancel culture' was appropriate responses to the sexual violence and abuse of public figures like R. Kelly and Bill Cosby," says Preston Mitchum, a civil rights activist and attorney. "Whenever multiple people are impacted by violence and life-altering events, I believe we must be comfortable investing in things that make us feel safer—and, sometimes, that thing is by canceling other people."

It's important to continually draw the line and distinguish what cancel culture is. The rise of online bullying and harassment in the name of disagreement has made many rush to blame cancel culture. There's been a wave of terrible stories, detailing how public figures receive harassment or even death threats as a result of online misconduct from trolls. Naturally, these attacks impact the victims' mental health. This was the case in February 2020 when British television presenter Caroline Flack of the hit show *Love*

Island committed suicide at the age of forty, following the public backlash to her assault of her boyfriend. At the time, some argued that the excessive online criticism spurred by cancel culture might have played a role in her demise. But Flack had a long history of mental illness and self-harm, and while being in the spotlight might have amplified her struggles, it's trivial and misleading to frame cancel culture as her motivation for taking her own life. The attacks and bullying of Flack cannot be considered cancel culture. She was not abusing her power, nor were those attacking her online oppressed or trying to get her to simply apologize. This was just straight-up cyberbullying, plain and simple.

As I mentioned in the introduction, R&B singer Chrisette Michele faced similar backlash after accepting $75,000 to perform during the presidential inauguration of Donald Trump in 2017. Hoping she could use the performance to "be a bridge" between Donald Trump and the Black community, Michele didn't expect public reaction to be so detrimental to her career and personal life. Michele claims that the criticism she faced, which included death threats, put her into a depression that played a part in her miscarriage. And while there were legitimate critiques of Michele's decision to participate in an event that celebrated one of the nation's most outwardly bigoted leaders, the reckless decision by some to attack her with death threats shouldn't be blamed on cancel culture. While Michele's performance was open for critique, those who called for her death aren't an accurate reflection of cancel culture—but another example of how some can easily conflate online harassment with cancel culture.

Just like depression and death, cyberbullying and harassment existed long before the term *cancel culture* went viral. Therefore, it is intellectually dishonest to suggest that cancel culture is causing such toxic behavior. According to this faulty logic, cyberbullying, death threats, and harassment have emerged because of cancel culture as well, when in reality, bullies have always been bullies. The fact of the matter is, when people call on others to boycott a person or institution, they're not responsible for those who take more dangerous measures.

Cancel culture is not cyberbullying someone to death, for such an act lacks the focus, thought process, and activism that is required of the former. Just like hate speech isn't free speech, simply attacking someone through unprincipled criminal activity isn't cancel culture, it's bullying. For example, when animal rights organization PETA goes to events and protests people who wear fur, that's a fair example of cancel culture. But when some of their supporters go as far as to throw red paint on individuals and physically assault them—that moves things into a realm of behavior that isn't cancel culture. The same can be said for the Black Lives Matter movement. The activists involved in nonviolent organizing and creating legitimate demands for police accountability aren't to be compared to individuals who burn down buildings and steal. There have been countless movements where some individuals have exploited the hard work of others for their own selfish gain. Cancel culture, just like other legitimate actions, is often exploited by bad actors looking to push their own agendas beyond the fair and legitimate critique of the activists involved. This has been going on since the beginning of time.

The rise of Antifa, the violent anti-fascist organization, is an example of cancel culture being exploited. The group's notoriety was at an all-time high during the racial uprisings of 2020, when several members, many of whom are white men, were seen on camera across various cities damaging property and causing chaos. Antifa claimed they were defending these neighborhoods against aggressive police tactics and alt-right extremist groups, such as the Proud Boys and the Oath Keepers. But in cities such as Portland, Oregon, several Black residents told the media that they weren't in favor of Antifa's presence and that their approach was diluting the nonviolent, anti-racism message they are in favor of. Consequently, conservative media outlets used the actions of Antifa to frame cancel culture as something that's gone too far—even conflating the Black Lives Matter activism with that of the troublesome group.

"These are acts of domestic terror," Trump said in a June 2020 speech[7] in the Rose Garden, during the George Floyd protests. The former president, desperate to blame progressives for anything during his contentious reelection campaign, tried to paint Black Lives Matter protesters and those who committed anarchist crimes with a broad brush as "radical-left, bad people," while ominously invoking Antifa alongside them. It should be noted that Trump gave this speech exactly moments before heavily armed troops and riot police advanced without warning on the largely peaceful Black Lives Matter protesters across the street from the White House. But after previously tweeting that he planned to designate Antifa as a terrorist organization, Trump was determined to double down on the misinformation—a tactic he's used many times before.

"The violence instigated and carried out by Antifa and other similar groups in connection with the rioting is domestic terrorism and will be treated accordingly," former U.S. attorney general William Barr claimed at the time. Yes, there had been violent acts that included property destruction and theft, along with reports of cops and activists having been seriously injured and killed. But the federal officials had offered little evidence[8] that proved Antifa was behind the Black Lives Matter movement that has inspired millions of Americans since the deaths of George Floyd and Breonna Taylor.

"Can't believe I have to say this, but here goes. Black Lives Matter and 'Antifa' are not the same thing," wrote *Washington Post* columnist Jonathan Capehart in a September 2020 op-ed.[9] "Let me repeat. Black Lives Matter and Antifa are not the same thing." Capehart ended his op-ed this way: "Remember that the next time someone tries to make Black Lives Matter and Antifa one and the same. They aren't. Anyone who insists that they are is misinformed at best and a willful liar at worst."

It's critical to make distinctions between cancel culture and smoke and mirrors that simply distract. If you're trying to distinguish between the two, here are some questions you can ask: Is it a stunt, or is it saying something more? Is it simply reckless violence, or is there a larger purpose behind the backlash? Is it co-opting a movement or starting a revolution? Is there cowardice among the messengers or a bold proclamation? How does this action affect the canceler's livelihood or existence? What part of their existence are they fighting for? Organizations and individuals like Antifa, anonymous hackers, cyberbullies, and trolls don't represent cancel culture—they are simply the perpetrators of unprincipled and irrational forms of dissent.

Who are the ones conflating violence with cancel culture and manipulating public opinion? Also, who opposes cancel culture? The answer is almost always: those with power. The powerful make and enforce laws, have an oversize influence on the distribution of wealth, and have greater freedoms than those with limited influence. There's a reason why politicians, celebrities, and influential public figures often lament about cancel culture—because the people who gave them their status, wealth, and privilege are the same ones that can use cancel culture to take it all away. Of course they hate cancel culture—why would they want to be held more accountable? Fearmongering around cancel culture is meant to encourage everyday people to stop doing it, because it is effective. It's not actually that difficult to discern between cancel culture and cyberbullying, but those with lots to lose would have you believe they are one and the same. Doxing, trolling, and online harassment are meant to hurt and silence, while cancel culture calls for change. Anytime the most influential are telling everyone to stop doing something, that should be a sign that it poses a threat to them—which is a good thing for those living on the margins.

Cancel culture is a redistribution of agency. When thousands of American college students from the late 1970s to mid-1980s actively urged their campuses to divest from apartheid South Africa—that wasn't a personal attack but an action based on a shift in moral values. After years of internal protest, international economic boycotts, and pressure from the West, the government of South Africa began to dismantle apartheid in 1990. In all aspects of cancel culture, control is what's being challenged more than individual people themselves. When you reframe cancel culture—regardless of the platform it exists on—as a matter of reassessing power within society, then it's easier to understand why so many with influence and control hate it so much and want you to reject it.

The racial uprisings of 2020 inspired a new wave of people to share their experiences with racism in the same way that victims of sexual abuse felt more comfortable speaking up during #MeToo. Social media provides an opportunity for everyday people to feel comfortable sharing experiences that would usually be disregarded when shared by other means—making it much less difficult to cancel someone in the process.

Prior to social media, the ability for individuals to collectively work to cancel a problematic individual or institution required more in-person coordination and strategy. If a politician said something offensive, you would have to write a letter to an editor and the news would hopefully pick it up, or you would try to coordinate a demonstration. But what if that editor didn't publish your note or enough people weren't available to attend your in-person protest? The chances of effecting immediate change were dim.

"The powerful do not have to act quickly on behalf of common folks," says education advocate Dr. Crystal M. Edwards. "The speed of their reactions aligns with who they deem important, usually in their circle. Cancel culture is a rapid response to political agendas for the sole purpose of grabbing the layman's attention in order to influence the masses."

The power of canceling now is that it doesn't require a zip code, letter to the editor, or some other outdated form of demonstration—it can happen immediately online at the drop of a social media post. This is why cancel culture grew in prominence, because it gave everyday people a way to share their grievances in real time and the ability to build consensus around an issue without delay.

"So, the thing about cancel culture is that to the extent that it is enabled by digital and social media technologies and the twenty-four-hour news cycle, there's no turning it off," says Meredith D. Clark, Ph.D., an associate professor in the College of Arts, Media, and Design at Northeastern University in Boston. "You cannot control it. You cannot control how people move, how they make demands, when and where they make those demands. That is necessary from my perspective as a recovering journalist, and specifically a newspaper journalist, because we know about the tricks and the techniques that powerful figures will use to avoid accountability in real time.

"We are familiar with the practice of issuing a press release about a major issue at five o'clock on Friday. Because government figures know that they can shut down the office and they don't have to answer to anyone until the weekend is over, like they don't have to worry about that on Monday. Social media breaks down that time barrier and says, 'No, no, no, you don't get to post this and just walk away.' It's like the inverse of throwing a bomb." While the weekends of old might have bought you time for people to forget a Friday announcement, social media means that announcement—or bomb—will be coming right back at you.

J. K. Rowling's anti-trans tweets[10] made her an instant target for cancellation in this way. The more that she doubled down on her beliefs around the "dangers" trans people represent to cis women and girls, the quicker the fury grew. Cast members of the *Harry Potter* movies, like Daniel Radcliffe, made statements apologizing for the hurt Rowling had caused. Earlier LGBTQIA activists did not have access to this kind of quick messaging. After several instances of police raiding the now iconic gay bar the Stonewall Inn, queer community members were fed up. On June 28, 1969, they physically fought back against the establishment that had oppressed them for living their truth. They were being attacked, and who could they ask for help? Not the police—they were the ones attacking. Legislation and public opinion were not yet on the side of the men in that bar. What happened that evening was more than dissent—it was a riot. It wasn't just about a bar but about the humanity of those whose sexuality and gender identity were treated as criminal. It was the people versus the police, heteronormative doctrine versus LGBTQIA liberation. The Stonewall riots were one of the boldest expressions of cancel culture as we understand it today because the LGBTQIA protesters were fighting against a violent police force to defend their identity and existence.

What would be birthed from that historical movement were legendary groups such as the Gay Activists Alliance and the Gay Liberation Front. These organizations, intentional in being out during a time when homosexuality and transgender visibility were outlawed, made the fight for LGBTQIA rights a major pillar of American politics. Had it not been for these brave activists, who were determined to call out and cancel mainstream homophobia where they saw it, LGBTQIA issues wouldn't have been a major talking point during presidential campaigns, in political party agendas, and in the mainstream media. The Gay Pride marches and parades we know today are a reminder to society that LGBTQIA individuals can't be easily canceled, for these people's existence serves to confront and end conservative norms that have tried to keep them in the closet for ages. Pride marches are so accepted now that progressive politicians like to be seen participating in them the same way a conservative politician might want to be seen at a Trump rally.

It's important to observe and differentiate how cancel culture is exhibited by both progressives and conservatives. Although their tactics and motivations are different, the drive and focus remain the same. For LGBTQIA activists, the cancellation of conservative bigots infringing upon their right to exist means liberation. For the freedom fighters of the mid-twentieth century, the end of Jim Crow laws meant equality. For Tea Party conservatives of the early 2010s, it meant trying to return America to its former leadership of white, Christian, cis-het dominance by seeking to cancel the social progress made by America's first Black president. As an out-of-power, extreme wing of the conservative party, the Tea Party waged PR campaigns in the media, [11] such as birtherism, to undermine Obama and his progressive agenda. All these various individuals and groups formulated around a plan to win—some succeeded, while others failed. But cancel culture isn't defined by wins or losses—it's defined by the sheer determination to pursue change.

"I think cancel culture is necessary any time an organization, person, or system that causes irreparable harm believes it is too big to fail," says activist J. Mase III. "People in power need to always understand they are not more powerful than the people. People like Supreme Court justice Brett Kavanaugh needed to be canceled. That cancellation by the people, in stark contrast to a system that upheld him—an alleged rapist—as the pinnacle of morality, proves just how immoral the U.S. government is."

Not all cancellations are successful. Brett Kavanaugh still sits on the Supreme Court, but that doesn't discount the effort that was made to stop his ascension. The conversations surrounding Kavanaugh and Christine Blasey Ford went beyond the details of their specific history and brought increased awareness to the complexities of sexual assault. There was a time when the consensus reaction to their story would have been "Boys will be boys" or "What did she expect?" Even though hearts and minds are changing around sexual assault, the power structure—a conservative majority at that time—was on Kavanaugh's side. Which is why cancel culture really was the only option. While cancel culture did not win the day in the Kavanaugh case, it did and does add to a discussion about sexual assault, power, and politics. Cancel culture, as we'll see over the next few chapters, can be cumulative—each cancellation acting like a brick in a wall that builds and builds toward progress.

WHEN PROGRESSIVES CANCEL

X X X X X X X X X X X X X X

The Left uses cancel culture to expand
rights and freedoms for more people.

All cancellations share a common DNA—that impulse to do away with something or someone that threatens the way of life of the canceler. But like gene expressions, the way cancellations play out can be as varied as humans, which is to say that there are limitless ways that people can use cancel culture if they meet the requirements discussed in the "Cancel Culture Been Here" chapter. Within that enormous set known as humans, there are large groups that act together, with similar goals and values. When it comes to cancel culture, two of the biggest, most obvious subsets are progressives and conservatives. The ways these ends of the political spectrum operate are starkly different, even if their essential goal is the same: to reject people or policies that do not align with their values. I'll start by looking at progressives.

On March 12, 2021, New York governor Andrew Cuomo finally had something to say. Once a darling of the Democratic Party, Cuomo was facing multiple allegations of sexual harassment from women who had worked for him over the years. Already having been criticized in the press following a federal investigation into underreporting COVID-19 deaths, Cuomo was in hot water. At that point, most New York House Democrats and the National Organization for Women were calling for him to resign. Losing progressive allies left and right, the longtime political heavyweight needed to say something—anything—that would address the mounting pressure he was facing to resign.

At a press conference, Cuomo went on the defense.[1] "People know the difference between playing politics, bowing to cancel culture, and the truth. Let the review proceed," he told the press during an abrupt phone briefing. "I am not going to resign. I was not elected by the politicians," Cuomo added to double down on his decision not to exit in disgrace. "I was elected by the people."

This was the first time a widely known elected liberal had directly blamed cancel culture for their sudden demise in office. Whereas Donald Trump and other Republicans had often made cancel culture the scapegoat for any backlash they received, it was uncommon to see leaders within the Democratic Party embrace such terminology as a defense. Most mainstream media frame cancel culture as being solely the province of the political Far Left. Today, it would come as no surprise to hear people frame cancel culture as something that progressives do as a form of protest. And while this is technically correct, this framing inaccurately positions cancel culture as a tool of the Left rather than a tool being used by both conservatives and progressives.

Cuomo knew what he was doing during that press briefing. Often viewed as a senior moderate in progressive spaces, the longtime politician was stoking division among colleagues who felt torn on whether to still support him. His not "bowing to cancel culture" was an attempt to exhibit strength against what he was framing as a witch hunt. Dodging questions about whether he had a consensual relationship with any of the women who accused him of sexual misconduct, Cuomo made society itself the focus of his defense. Rather than take any accountability in the heat of the moment, he chose to point the finger at his critics—those whom he felt were trying to ruin him via this new online weapon called cancel culture.

This was a major departure for a governor who had made it a point to stand up to Trump's antics during the global pandemic. Now temporal use he joined the former president in being yet another politician who'd been accused by multiple women of sexual harassment and tried to deflect. He also shared Trump's play of blaming cancel culture for his troubles. Both men tried to frame cancel culture as the boogeyman, born from the mob mentality of progressives wanting to enforce political correctness.

By invoking cancel culture in his decision not to resign, Cuomo attempted to make himself the victim of his own scandal. He instantly vilified his accusers and those who believed them—the very progressives who once joined him in his criticism of Trump. No one would be surprised by a politician doing anything they could to maintain their status. What was somewhat surprising was watching progressives call for Cuomo's resignation while he maintained his innocence. Why would liberal voices fight among each other? Didn't they see conservatives on Fox News enjoying the catfight? You can imagine conservatives laughing it up: "The Left is so enamored of cancel culture, they're doing it to themselves!" *This wasn't how any of this was supposed to work.*

Except progressives have often been willing to cancel their own—even the most powerful—when they feel it's appropriate. Conservatives are typically loyal to each other when under attack, and the driving forces behind *who* and *why* they cancel are starkly different from progressives. Progressives have been, and continue to be, far more willing to cancel within their own political group. For example, liberals like Cuomo, Harvey Weinstein, and Bill Clinton were highly popular until their actions violated core progressive values of women's rights. When progressives cancel, they typically do so based on a moral litmus test that is rooted in identity politics.

"Without a doubt, there are progressive movements that attempt to hold accountable powerful people who harmed others," says Kenyette Tisha Barnes, notable lobbyist and lecturer, who is also the cofounder of the

#MuteRKelly movement. "In addition, the calls to hold accountable notable men who used their power and influence to commit decades of sexual assault and abuse. Harvey Weinstein, Bill Cosby, and of course R. Kelly are examples." These "contemporary movements" Barnes describes are cancel culture by another name, and it's notable that most of the pressure to cancel Weinstein, Cosby, and Kelly came from progressive spaces. If things were reversed, and these men were conservative rather than progressive, it's not hard to imagine conservatives defending them in accordance with the way they typically utilize identity politics. In fact, we don't have to imagine it—Fox News broadcasts these defenses regularly for conservative figures, most famously Donald Trump.

Progressives being willing to call out their own expands beyond individuals to policy—even when that policy was created by their own side. President Clinton enacted "Don't Ask, Don't Tell" in 1993. DADT was U.S. military policy between 1994 and 2011 that allowed closeted homosexuals to serve, so long as they did not, in any way, make their queerness known. It also barred senior officers from making any inquiries into soldiers' private lives, while banning openly gay servicepeople. Initially framed to allow homosexuals to serve in the army, it was quickly seen as being another kind of ban. The call to end DADT was based on giving LGBTQIA people in the military basic human rights. President Obama signed legislation to drop the ban in 2011. It was one progressive canceling another progressive's imperfect effort. The focus was progress, not holding on to the status quo.

"Progressives often cancel to disrupt unchecked cycles of abuse. The conduct of the individual or organization in question, and the impact of their poor conduct, is central to the cancellation," says Dorcas Adedoja, a Black transmasculine activist and Human Rights Campaign ACTIVATE fellow. "Conservatives cancel and advocate for their own personal ways of life to be the only options available to the public." Adedoja makes an important distinction here: Progressives are willing to fight for the rights of all people, not only themselves. Obama didn't cancel DADT to defend his own way of life but understood that others should enjoy his cis-het privilege. In other words, progressives want to move things forward—for everyone—and conservatives want to keep them the same or go back to "the good ol' days."

As I mentioned in the previous chapter, the progressive departure from American conformity began decades ago during the countercultural movement, which began in the 1950s. Progressive values as we know them today were born in an era that was all about youth rejecting the cultural standards previously enforced by their parents. Before boomers were being okayed by millennials and Gen Zers, they were once the defiant rebels who wanted more than the provincial life America was giving them. Racial segregation, strict, patriarchal child-rearing, and other forms of rigid conformity made a younger generation anxious for change.

To be clear, white boomers of that time were the social litmus test for how progressive the country was becoming. They were not, however, the spark behind such changes. Black and Brown Americans had more evolved views on social issues, such as racial integration, labor rights, women's rights, and immigration rights, long before their white counterparts did. Until that time, social inequality was more overtly about Black versus white due to the legislation of oppressive Jim Crow laws. The most marginalized Americans originated the nation's current progressive movement. It was their reshaping of cancel culture that gave white people a voice to amplify social issues they didn't always champion.

The civil rights movement is the most consequential social protest in U.S. history. What took place in the 1950s and 1960s was nothing short of the golden era of cancel culture. Focused, determined, and committed, Black progressives and their allies executed a plan to desegregate America by nonviolent means. Their decision made them outlaws and outcasts at the time, but their mission was to give a subset of the nation basic human dignity and equal rights. If activists had not called for the cancellation of institutions and practices white people held in high regard at the time, society as we know it would have continued to be oppressive toward much of the population.

When Rosa Parks, a Black woman, refused to give up her seat at the front of a bus to a white man in Montgomery, Alabama, in 1955, her defiance signaled the beginning of a new movement. Jim Crow laws in the South made a predominately Black bus ridership sit in the back seats. Parks said no. Her bold refusal was an act of civil disobedience that placed her in jail, and her protest sparked the Montgomery bus boycotts, in which Black Americans refused to ride all city buses. For 381 days, Black people rejected buses in favor of walking, bikes, and every other way to get around. Buses weren't being canceled because they weren't good modes of transportation but because their rules were dehumanizing. Forcing Black people to sit in the back of a bus simply because of the color of their skin was institutionalized white supremacy. The gross incarceration of those who detested such policies served as a wake-up call to America of its double standards. A nation that was pushing for democracy on the world stage was suppressing the rights of their own citizens back at home.

After the bus company that booted Parks was nearly bankrupted, the Supreme Court stepped in to rule that racial segregation on any form of transportation was against the law—which influenced the city of Montgomery to immediately prohibit such discrimination on their buses as well. The decision of Black activists to economically divest from a racist institution had finally paid off.

Progressive cancel culture at that moment had granted the civil rights movement a major victory.

Sit-ins that empowered Black Americans to protest in public spaces signified the end of one form of cancel culture and the birth of another. Jim Crow laws that were intended to segregate Black people from the rest of the country were essentially cancel culture, because white supremacists who pushed such policies were legislatively canceling the presence of Black people. Signs that read "No Blacks Allowed" were telling people of color that they were deliberately canceled by a society that valued whiteness. Progressives countered this by resisting the norms that had been set during the Reconstruction era of half-assing America's commitment to freeing enslaved people. They valued expanded rights over conformity and counterpunched these acts of bigotry and racial discrimination by actively canceling the individuals and institutions that perpetuated hate.

Led by Dr. Martin Luther King Jr., the civil rights movement set the standard for American progressive identity. It was no longer socially acceptable to express explicitly racist rhetoric. You could not claim to be a progressive if you still believed in a "separate but equal" society. Those were the new terms. In the same way, it also set the standard for American conservative identity. These identities as we know them today were being established by the principles set during the countercultural movement.

An October 2018 study[2] published in *American Economic Review* confirmed that "racially conservative" white Americans in the South began to leave the Democratic Party to become Republicans in the early 1950s, following Democratic president Harry Truman's support for civil rights initiatives in the late 1940s. These departures only increased after another Democratic president, Lyndon B. Johnson, signed the 1964 Civil Rights Act, which officially prohibited discrimination based on race, color, religion, sex, or national origin. It was during this time that the Democratic Party, largely backed by progressives, became the party of a liberal, civil rights agenda. Economic professors Ilyana Kuziemko and Ebonya Washington, who were the authors of the study, described former president John F. Kennedy Jr.'s first proposal to outlaw racial discrimination in public accommodations as being "the critical moment when Civil Rights is, for the first time, an issue of great salience to the majority of Americans and an issue clearly associated with the Democratic Party." In other words, distinction between Republicans and Democrats as conservatives and liberals, respectively, had finally emerged and solidified.

Once a progressive identity had been set, the success of the civil rights movement inspired several social causes to finally have their revolutions. In 1965, after Filipino American farmworkers went on strike against grape growers in the Delano region of California, a new alliance was formed. The United Farm Workers of America, a group cocreated by marginalized workers and the National Farm Workers Association, led by activist Cesar Chavez, implemented tactics from both Gandhi's Salt March and the Montgomery bus boycott. This time around, activist farmers were canceling grapes to put pressure on table- and wine-grape growers to pay them more after years of being denied better working conditions. Chavez mobilized not only farmers but the public to join in the boycott of Delano grapes over exploitative labor practices. It took years, but with the public committed to leaving non-union-picked grapes rotting on the shelves, a collective bargaining agreement was reached in 1970. As a result, over ten thousand farmworkers received better pay, bene-fits, and working conditions that wouldn't have come had it not been for cancel culture.

But not all forms of cancel culture during this era were nonviolent. As I described in the "When Canceling Was the Only Option" chapter, on June 28, 1969, a riot broke out at the Stonewall Inn in Greenwich Village af-ter a group of diverse LGBTQIA activists fought against the police who had constantly raided the venue and at-tacked them. Although the riot lasted for three days, there wasn't any major press coverage of the incident at the time. However, word of mouth from the activists who were there on Christopher Street on those nights helped ignite the nation's LGBTQIA movement. During this era, this tenacious group of queer and nonbinary rebels— and those who supported them—would go on to boycott

Florida orange juice and Coors beer, following the rise of the Christian Right and its anti-gay spokespeople Anita Bryant and Joseph Coors,[3] respectively. Bryant, a minor celebrity of the late 1960s, rose to fame as the face of juice from the Sunshine State, with her commercial claiming, "A day without orange juice is like a day without sunshine." When anti-discrimination laws were about to be passed in Florida, Bryant was at the forefront of the opposition. She used her national platform to fearmonger about the harm that homosexuals could do to children. Gay and lesbian activists decided to hit back with a boycott—they called it a "gaycott"—against OJ. Gay bars—and some non-gay bars—across the country stopped serving orange juice in their cocktails and T-shirts with anti-Bryant slogans like SQUEEZE ANITA and A DAY WITHOUT HUMAN RIGHTS IS LIKE A DAY WITHOUT SUNSHINE became popular. Although Bryant did lose her position with the Florida orange juice commission, the anti-discrimination legislation bill was voted down. Still, the protests elevated the visibility of LGBTQIA people in America and inspired a new generation of activists. These efforts would establish this group of marginalized Americans as a force to be reckoned with, as many of their major legislative victories would come in the twenty-first century.

Queer activism during the countercultural movement was in alignment with the sexual revolution and hippie spirit at the time. Sex, drugs, and rock and roll were embraced by young boomers, who were also anti-war and all about canceling conformity. Long hair, nudity, psychedelic drugs, and peace sign symbols of the Summer of Love were essentially a big middle finger to the America of the early twentieth century. The embrace of the Black Panthers and their anti-capitalism rhetoric could be felt in this new wave of intercultural alliances that demanded better labor rights and social justice for all. Canceling the Vietnam War, legalizing abortion, and federally granting women equal rights were on the agenda.

Things were moving fast, and American progressive culture felt unstoppable. The boycotts, riots, protests, and diverse coalitions were demanding an entire deconstruction of old American values. Canceling racism, ending sexism, and abolishing exploited labor were fair calls of action. People of color, women, LGBTQIA people, migrant workers, and those who felt they were on the margins finally had a platform to express themselves. The Civil Rights Act of 1964 had finally given them the opportunity to feel more comfortable speaking out. But as all good things must come to an end, so did the countercultural movement.

There is no other honest way to explain why an era that was pushing some of America's most progressive values faltered without simply pointing the finger: white America. White people—cisgender, straight, and Christian— wanted their country back. The progressive era, to them, was a regressive decline in the country's moral decency and standard of socioeconomic living. Rather than look at the improved quality of life of other demographics of people, they pointed to the excessive drug use and relaxed sexual mores. Sexual liberation, to conservatives, was vulgarity and promiscuity, LGBTQIA visibility was immoral fornication, abortion was murder, and diversity, overstepping its social boundaries. The 1980s saw the cultural pendulum swing back to conservatism. With the late Ronald Reagan as their presidential beacon of hope, the Right thought they had finally made their case to "Make America Great Again." The slogan, first used during Reagan's presidential campaign, perfectly described the conservative cancel culture movement and their longing to return to the simplicity of the 1950s. Whereas progressives canceled to revolutionize, conservatives canceled to restore. The restoration of America to conservatives meant a return to the country that their lily-white, patriarchal, Bible-thumping politics would thrive within.

The 1980s and 1990s would become an embrace between conservatism and moderate/centrist values. Protests and boycotts took place on the progressive side, but things weren't the same. Many of the notable revolutionaries of the 1960s and 1970s were either imprisoned, assassinated, or culturally irrelevant at this point. Skyrocketing AIDS cases killed millions of LGBTQIA Americans, and crack cocaine ravaged Black and Brown communities—both crises faced a lack of empathy from the Reagan administration. Most of the flames from the countercultural movement sparked by the end of the Vietnam War had burned out due to Reagan's ultraconservatism, George H. W. Bush's problematic foreign policies, and moderate/centrist Bill Clinton's anti-LGBTQIA "Don't Ask, Don't Tell" policy and devastating 1994 Crime Bill. The war on drugs destroyed diverse communities that once had potential. Mass incarceration crippled a generation of formerly free Black and Brown people. The NAACP during this time struggled financially, with some of its most ardent supporters questioning its future. Progressive values as we had previously established them were mainly being expressed in the most marginalized facets of society and pop culture.

White America, and some diverse middle-class Americans, saw economic strides while the rest of society suffered. The great political compromise of the 1990s was due to the three-term presidential reign of conservative presidents. After Reagan successfully led a fierce conservative takeover of American values that guaranteed his less-favored vice president, George H. W. Bush, would have the chance to succeed him, the Democratic Party establishment needed a game changer. Clinton was their perfect storm, given his moderate appeal and centrist politics. This was a man who could win the unflinching love of Black voters, while surreptitiously pushing for policies that would harm them just as much as Reagan's had. But this era of neoliberalism re-shifted identity politics in even more disingenuous ways.

As I stated, progressive cancel culture wasn't as robust in comparison to previous decades: We saw the anti-apartheid movement conclude, aggressive public activism against AIDS decline, and heated debate against music censorship fizzle out. Democrats, less progressive than ever, had officially played into the "lesser evil" role compared with conservatives. Whereas Kennedy and Johnson had taken bold strides in pushing for civil rights, Democrats of this new era simply had to reform the more aggressive policies of their opposition to appear more moderate. Reagan and Bush had swung the pendulum so far right that Clinton's centrist approach could appear progressive. We see a version of this moderate/centrist grip on progressive cancel culture in President Joe Biden's current call for police reform, something his conservative counterparts find too radical—but it's nothing like calls from progressives to defund the police. Vice President Kamala Harris, a Black and Indian woman, refused to call America a racist nation—but agreed with her moderate leader that racism must be "rooted" out.

The moderate/centrist grip on progressive cancel culture finally came to a screeching halt once the new millennium ushered in Republican president George W. Bush. Bush, the rebellious son of the last Republican president to hold the office before him, reset how all cancel culture would take off in the digital era. After the horrific terrorist attacks on September 11, 2001, America entered the war on terror. This era led to the unfair profiling of Muslim Americans and the violation of citizens' privacy. A rebirth of mainstream liberal American outrage also took off. In 2004, the controversial documentary *Fahrenheit 9/11*[4] drove progressive sentiment to cancel Bush's run at a second term. Academy Award–winning filmmaker Michael Moore used his public platform to call out the president's handling of the war on terrorism, as well as his overall ineffectiveness. This would be complemented by a rise in progressive celebrities publicly bashing Bush and mobilizing the public to vote against him. Although it claimed to be nonpartisan, there was no doubt that hip-hop mogul Sean "Diddy" Combs's Citizen Change movement[5] calling on young people to "Vote or Die" was a shot at Bush's reelection efforts. Despite the collective efforts, Bush went on to defeat Democratic moderate John Kerry in November 2004.

Within a couple of years, social media was born, and with it, the new wave of progressive cancel culture that we currently live in had finally arrived. The emergence of the social influencer—a person who amasses a great following on a nontraditional platform—as well as the birth of the viral video, would become the quintessential assets for progressives and their canceling efforts in the years to come. Driven by identity politics, the options to hold problematic individuals and institutions accountable would feel limitless compared to those of previous generations. Whereas progressives of the twentieth century were more strategic and reliant on in-person demonstrations and petitioning, as well as receiving coverage on legacy media, technology had now changed the game. The rise of social media platforms such as Facebook, YouTube, and Twitter in the late 2000s would help give the nation's first Black president, Barack Obama, a millennial voter advantage—setting the stage for a progressive cancel culture expansion.

The previous era of formal conservatism died with Obama's election. What would come years later would be Far Right extremism, a movement so unprecedented in recent history it would make many political analysts reconsider how terrible Bush had been when compared to Trump. For progressives, Obama felt like a major step in the right direction for a country that was beginning to lose its way on the global stage. They had forever wanted anyone who was not a white, cisgender, heterosexual male to be president, and their dreams finally came true. This fresh new political era validated and emboldened a new generation of millennials, who were now able to vote and cancel via social media.

The first sign of progressive cancel culture as we currently know it took place on March 5, 2012. A YouTube video produced[6] by a small nonprofit called Invisible Children made the world aware of, and hate, Joseph Kony, a Ugandan warlord who abducted children by the thousands for two decades. Even worse, he abused them and used them as soldiers and sex slaves. Nobody could have ever imagined that a thirty-minute video would help raise $32 million and appeal to such influencers as Bill Gates, Rihanna, and even Oprah Winfrey to spread awareness. The desire to catch—and cancel—Kony was so rampant that even the U.S. government was pressured to boost military operations on the ground in Uganda. Sadly, none of this would be enough to capture Kony, and the warlord remains on the loose. But it did demonstrate the power of social media to quickly mobilize progressives around issues on a global scale, even while Invisible Children came under intense scrutiny for their handling of donated funds.

Such digital mobilization on a viral, global scale reached new heights the following year with the emergence of the Black Lives Matter movement in 2013. The viral hashtag #BlackLivesMatter single-handedly changed how we would consider activism, race, and social media in the twenty-first century. Black Twitter users were activated by the acquittal of George Zimmerman for killing Trayvon Martin, an unarmed Black teen, in February 2012. The three Black women cofounders who started the movement, Alicia Garza, Patrisse Cullors, and Opal Tometi, not only used it to spread public awareness—but also to inspire work on the ground. In the following years, the hashtag encouraged grassroots activism calling for justice for the extrajudicial police killings of Michael Brown, Eric Garner, Tamir Rice, Tony McDade, and countless others. Black intersectional community leaders and scholars, such as Dr. Kimberlé Crenshaw, incorporated the hashtag #SayHerName within the movement, to avoid erasure of the police violence and racial profiling faced by Black women like Sandra Bland, India Kager,

Korryn Gaines, Breonna Taylor, and others. These stances would reshape how society would critique policing and its impact on Black people.

Black Lives Matter is the civil rights movement of the modern information era. Unlike the previous civil rights movement of the twentieth century, the activists involved are more decentralized and less attuned to a hierarchical structure. Whereas the NAACP, Urban League, Black Panther Party, and others had their presidents, boards, and chairpersons, the Black Lives Matter movement prides itself on being accessible to practically anyone who believes in its cause. With a national network of activists that span over thirty local chapters across America, leadership is more about individualistic expression than conformity—a major contrast to the era in which such social justice movements were born.

For Black Lives Matter, the cancellation of rigid police structures that operate with no real accountability drives its focus. To supporters, police aren't allies, rather they are operating within a system of racism that seeks to enforce more harm than safety. By exposing the shocking amount of state-sanctioned violence against people of color, along with racial profiling, Black Lives Matter makes the case that community conversations, reform measures, or even apologies are inadequate. BLM posits that what is required is an institutional overhaul of the criminal justice system as we know it. Such ambitions don't go without pushback. Before the major racial uprisings of 2020, national public opinion of the movement was net negative. Many found the activists to be too divisive, polarizing, and aggressive. Commentators on conservative news outlets like Fox News had likened them to the radical activists of the Black Panther Party and tried to dismiss their calls for justice as misplaced rage.

Following the increased visibility of the movement, several counterprotest movements formed as a response. The Blue Lives Matter movement was created by law enforcement leaders in 2014 to push for the murders of cops to be treated as hate crimes. They saw Black Lives Matter as an attack on their safety, one that was fueled more by hate than accountability. Such pro-police interests in canceling Black Lives Matter were accompanied by a rise of white supremacy. The White Lives Matter movement also took off to center white people's frustrations on the current critiques of racism. Listed as an official hate group by the Southern Poverty Law Center in 2016, this group would later have its slogan chanted out by torch-wielding alt-right protesters in 2017 during the infamous Unite the Right rally in Charlottesville, Virginia. Cancel culture found itself in the eye of the ideological storm. Those who were Black and progressive were likely to support changing the system of policing. Those who were white and conservative would beg to differ. But this was never a real debate. Groups such as Blue Lives Matter, and especially White Lives Matter, do not wish to engage in an intellectual discussion about BLM values. In fact, they seek to oversimplify the complex ideas and systems that make Black Lives Matter necessary. They use the cultural confusion around what BLM is about, to say things they could never have said before BLM existed. Imagine if someone had said white lives matter before the Ferguson protests of 2014? The Blue and White Lives Matter groups were co-opting and misrepresenting Black Lives Matter in a kind of whataboutism that tried to muddy the water rather than truly engage.

Accountability was, and is, driving the framework of modern progressive cancel culture. Previous iterations demanded change, called for reform, and desired a revolution altogether—but accountability is bigger than just a tangible action. While current progressive activists do desire changes that have been demanded in the past, they also want those who perpetuated such harms to pay. It's not enough to simply fix an issue and let bygones be bygones—progressives today are calling for swift action that addresses both the problem and the individual/institution that caused it.

The rise of the #MeToo movement highlights this transformation clearly. Originally a phrase used by activist Tarana Burke[7] in the early 2000s as a call to end sexual abuse and sexual harassment, the #MeToo movement was elevated to new heights following the downfall of Hollywood mogul Harvey Weinstein in 2017, as I discussed in the "When Canceling Was the Only Option" chapter. Weinstein, one of the most powerful men in the entertainment industry at the time, was accused and later convicted of sexually assaulting numerous women in the business. On social media, victims of sexual abuse and harassment used the hashtag #MeToo to signal how common these issues were in society. Then actress Alyssa Milano posted on Twitter that "if all the women who have been sexually harassed or assaulted wrote 'Me too' as a status, we might give people a sense of the magnitude of the problem." Since her post, #MeToo has been used over twenty million times on Twitter. This simple action helped reshape both our understanding of abuse and inspire a new wave of cancel culture.

Since that tweet, hundreds of men across various industries have been called out publicly and held accountable for their indecent ways. Hollywood heavyweight Bill Cosby was criminally convicted for sexual abuse. Both Cosby and Weinstein, along with Oscar-winning director Roman Polanski, were expelled from the Academy of Motion Picture Arts and Sciences. The mounting accusations and revelations of sexual misconduct led to dozens of abusers of power being fired. In 2019, *The New York Times* reported[8] that over two hundred men had lost their jobs or an acting role for being involved in a #MeToo scandal, with nearly half of their positions being filled by women. The swift reaction from society was a long time coming for a movement against sexual harassment that started long before hashtags were even thought of.

The fundamental focus behind canceling these men was to reduce harm to potential future victims and set an example for other would-be abusers. While some may pity the men who lost their careers, it's more important to consider what they did while they had them. The #Me-Too movement amplified survivors' voices and abusers' accountability in ways that more nuanced issues, such as systemic racism, still struggle with. The movement showcased the conflict between gender, class, and status within a microcosm (in this case, Hollywood) in a way that spotlighted the larger implications for society. For example, understanding the way that gender has always informed power made it easier for progressives and feminists to target the status quo. Men, like white people in the Black Lives Matter movement, hold the power and privilege in this scenario. By challenging the ways they exerted such positions in society, the movement was able to successfully expose and cancel many of those who violated trust. This was what accountability looked like by the end of 2019.

Progressive cancel culture eventually evolved past the confines of political party allegiance. Both the Black Lives Matter and the #MeToo movements showed the limitations of political parties' abilities to be effective in the cause. When Democratic presidential nominee Hillary Clinton ran in 2016, she was confronted by Black Lives Matter activists for her backing of the 1994 Crime Bill, which furthered the "tough on crime" presence of police officers and mass incarceration of Black men and women. Americans saw similar questions raised around the Democratic presidential ticket in 2020, when Joe Biden and Kamala Harris were challenged by progressives about their stances on law enforcement. Black Lives Matter activists have also critiqued members within their own movement whom they felt were afflicting harm or distracting from its mission. In 2019, a group of Black activists, scholars, journalists, and community members put out an open letter calling for activist Shaun King[9] to "sit down" after numerous allegations of bullying and doxing had resurfaced. These moments could be considered textbook examples of "progressives canceling their own," but they're deeper than that. They prove how activists on this side of the political spectrum place accountability over allegiance.

The #MeToo movement also held so-called progressives to account. We saw this in 2017, when Minnesota Democratic senator Al Franken resigned following allegations of unwanted touching. Franken, who was a longtime liberal favorite and former *Saturday Night Live* comic, was accused by Los Angeles radio host Leeann Tweeden of kissing her "aggressively" while they rehearsed a scene during a 2006 tour to entertain American troops in the Middle East and Afghanistan. Tweeden also released the photo that would become forever associated with Franken—him pretending to grope a sleeping Tweeden. After activists and thirty-six of his colleagues demanded that he step down due to the backlash, it sent a message loud and clear that progressives favored idealism over individuals—regardless of whether that person had a legislative history aligned with their own. Many years after his presidency, society now judges Bill Clinton for abusing his power during his sexual affair with then intern Monica Lewinsky. Once publicly slut-shamed and blamed for the affair, progressives now view Lewinsky as the victim of a scandal that was not just about sex—but about how powerful men can manipulate. Through her 2015 TED Talk, Lewinsky uncanceled[10] herself. When "The Price of Shame" went viral, it caused many to reconsider her story. Progressives realized that Lewinsky had no business taking the fall for a former president's act of public betrayal. Instances like these prove that protecting the individuality and decency of people means more to progressives than upholding institutions and the statuses of public figures.

"And so with so many different directions in this big tent of being liberal or progressive, the fighting gets messy, and it gets very personal because there's not a central narrative for all of us to cling to," says Meredith D. Clark, Ph.D. "And that, to me, is the major difference between canceling when conservatives do it versus canceling when progressives do it: There is a central message for conservatives to ground themselves in and to connect around—no central message for liberals. Progressives exist because we embrace differences, it is ultimately our strength and our weakness."

This is why powerful men like Andrew Cuomo can be canceled by the very progressives who once applauded his efforts during the pandemic. Within progressive cancel culture, there exists the ability to know that two things can be true at once. Cuomo can be a person who has supported liberal causes that have advanced the rights of women, LGBTQIA, immigrants, and people of color—while also being someone capable of alleged sexual misconduct. Just as Bill Clinton helped thousands of Black families in America receive necessary government assistance, he also pushed policies that led to them being more likely to be incarcerated than their white counterparts. Progressives, unlike conservatives, understand that canceling the things and people who cause harm isn't without nuance. Whereas conservatives often remain loyal to a fault to those who abuse their power so long as they're in agreement on political issues, progressives demand and expect more from their leaders. The "practice what you preach" litmus test is what drives the progressive agenda more than that of conservatives, because progressives are striving to formulate a more inclusive collective.

Conservatives don't have to subscribe to such considerations. Driven by their religion and patriotism, they base their code of canceling on maintaining institutions and powerful leaders that rule over them. God, America, the Bible, the church, and the Constitution are the fundamental customs that define how they act. Their decision to cancel LGBTQIA rights, sexual freedom, feminism, Black

Lives Matter, and other progressive values will always be rooted in something related to either their faith and/or patriotism. Right or wrong, they believe these issues impact their way of life. Watch a right-wing pundit on cable news or attend a Republican rally and attempt to get a few minutes in without hearing some commentary on God and/or America. Meanwhile, progressives recognize a society that isn't rooted in such narrow conformity, and they strive to be more aware of finding coexistence that's invested in maintaining humanity for all. Progressives are socially motivated to champion for the most marginalized—those who aren't the most accepted, defended, and amplified. Progressive cancel culture is about combating those who would further this suppression. Whereas conservatives cancel based on their religious self-righteousness, progressives cancel on their sense of utilitarianism.

"Progressives protect marginalized people more passionately, and they're more likely to use legitimate research and facts to back up their reasoning, even if they're nasty in the methods they use," says journalist William Ketchum III. "Conservative people don't concern themselves with facts when they're seeking to cancel someone; most important is that their base will either believe what they're saying or willingly spread it regardless of how they feel."

The contrast between progressive and conservative cancellations can be neatly summed up by the events surrounding one man: Colin Kaepernick. The decision by progressive activists to boycott the National Football League in 2016 was bigger than the world of sports. When former NFL quarterback Colin Kaepernick was blackballed for protesting police brutality and racial inequality in America, the conversation folded together two major issues. First, Kaepernick, a Black man, used his huge platform to call out the nation's racism. By deciding to take a knee during the national anthem, a visible sign of disrespect to many conservatives, he was making Americans question their own values in the fight for racial justice. The second conversation became about his right as an American to practice free speech. When Kaepernick went unsigned through the off-season and 2017 training camps, many saw this as a blatant sign of retaliation from the league for his outspoken activism. How could a Black man be publicly penalized for speaking out against a system that oppresses him? Wasn't such blackballing confirming the very racism that inspired him to take a knee in the first place?

Conservatives deflected the conversation from the disregard for Black lives and police violence against Black people toward their preferred subject of respecting patriotic symbols, such as the American dream, flag, and anthem. It was in this national debate that it became clear to me that modern-day cancel culture could be a double-edged sword that shifted based on identity politics. It was like one of those silly drawings where some people see a rabbit and some see a duck. Those who were in favor of Kaepernick's protest were most likely younger, more diverse, and progressive. Those who were against it were usually older, white, and conservative.

Let's be clear—there is nothing inherently unpatriotic in not standing for the anthem. That's each person's individual right. Allegiance to the flag is so baked into American culture that it can feel extreme to resist it. As still in-office president Barack Obama said at the time,[11] "Well, as I've said before, I believe that honoring our flag and our anthem is part of what binds us together as a nation. But I also always try to remind folks that part of what makes this country special is that we respect people's rights to have a different opinion. The test of our fidelity to our Constitution, to freedom of speech, to our Bill of Rights, is not when it's easy, but when it's hard. We fight sometimes so that people can do things that we disagree with. If they're doing it within the law, then we can voice our opinion objecting to it, but it's also their right."

With those words, Obama reiterated how progressives cancel in America today. Even if he didn't call what Kaepernick was doing *cancel culture,* he was, despite not realizing it, supporting it. Progressives don't cancel out of duty to their faith and nation but *despite* it. It's not about their blind allegiance to domestic sovereignty but a belief that others should be able to exist freely in a society that has historically oppressed them. They cancel as an act of protest against a suppression of humanity. Kaepernick being blackballed was a punishment for his choice to call for the end of police violence against Black people. If that meant defying the institution of law enforcement as we know it, many progressives didn't care, because they value individuals over institutions.

Cancel culture is a battle between conformity and revolution. Conservatives are nostalgic about the "good ol' days," when America was on top of the world. Their understanding of society back then is one where the nuclear family thrived because of their Judeo-Christian values. When the countercultural movement emerged, it was viewed as a disruption of normality and unity. To conservatives, discussions of race, gender, and sexuality were divisive—identity politics that were considered an abomination. At this point, it should come as no surprise that the whitest, straightest, most religious, and most American of the population subscribed to these ideals more than their more diverse counterparts. Conservative cancel culture has always been typically more invested in upholding ideals of white supremacy, religious dogma, and xenophobia than its progressive counterparts. And yet, many once-progressive notions have been embraced by countless contemporary mainstream conservatives, like access to birth control, gun safety laws, even same-sex marriage. The 2016 presidential election of Donald Trump felt like a regressive return to America's yesteryear, particularly when it followed the leadership of America's first Black commander in chief, but really, it was just a continuation of the trend of conservative cancel culture.

Trump's ultraconservative doctrine that sought to cancel diversity, equity, and inclusion across various political and social policies conflicted with the natural progression of society outside of Far Right circles. Unlike in the early twentieth century, Americans are now more sexually open, diverse, educated, and digital across the board. Regardless of political affiliation, society is collectively more tolerant and accepting of each other publicly than previous generations were. Progressive cancel culture in the 1960s helped speed this up, even though the Civil Rights Act of 1964 was not as successful as was hoped, and regardless of how activists were overly ambitious in their attempt to transform the entire system following the Civil Rights Act of 1964, their impact can still be felt today.

We see this in the continued advancement of all the major pillars that the countercultural movement sought to advance decades ago. Today, LGBTQIA people are federally allowed to get married and face less workplace discrimination. Following the racial uprisings of 2020, support and public opinion of Black Lives Matter has been growing in popularity. There are now more companies revitalizing their anti–sexual harassment policies and enforcing tougher sanctions for misconduct following the #MeToo movement than ever. As criminal justice reform, immigration rights, gun control, and fair workplace initiatives are consistent issues being debated in the public eye, the progressive agenda has been undeniably potent. The movement's ability to show progress over the decades is a testament of its fierce ability to cancel the very institutional barriers that once seemed invincible. Whereas conservatives seem to challenge the forward motion of time, progressives have history on their side.

The sign of the times is the advantage that progressive culture has utilized despite the sporadic insertion of conservative waves since the Reagan era of the 1980s. While there's been an increase in hate crimes following the rise of Trumpian politics and alt-right movements, society bends toward Left-leaning cultural norms. Demographics are not in conservatives' favor. For example, America's population will be a majority non-white by 2045. For white nationalists who uplifted conservative values as a defense mechanism to offset the changing tides of society, this proves to be another sign of defeat. Of course, people of color are not a monolith, and many vote and act in ways that may seem to be against their own interests. Yes, there were Black and Hispanic Trump voters—even in 2020—and misinformation campaigns and voter suppression continue to try to quash non-white democratic participation. Even still, these campaigns were not enough to get Trump reelected. The active failings of white supremacy, and its dominance masked as patriotism, serve as more indication of how powerful progressive cancel culture has become. Although there's still much progress that's left to be achieved, one thing is for certain: The slow self-demise of American conservatism—their numbers are falling as the country becomes increasingly diverse—has helped progressive cancel culture accelerate much easier than what could have ever been imagined by early freedom fighters.

WHEN CONSERVATIVES CANCEL

The Right uses cancel culture to retain power—and to keep others from acquiring it—by employing a myopic nostalgia for "the good ol' days."

The war on cancel culture reached new heights during the 2020 Republican National Convention. Staunch conservatives at the event warned voters that cancel culture was a threat to democracy and American values. Rather than present a policy platform, the convention focused on the "dangers" of progressives and tried to paint them as immoral, unpatriotic, anti-cop, and anti-American.

Nick Sandmann was a star of the show. The Kentucky high school student became known after a video of his interaction with a Native American activist in Washington, D.C., went viral. Initial video clips presented Sandmann,[1] with his red MAKE AMERICA GREAT AGAIN hat and a curt smile, as a troll harassing the activist. Additional video footage provided more context and showed that Sandmann had not started an already-heated confrontation. The narrative changed, and he eventually settled lawsuits against CNN and *The Washington Post*.

Sandmann became the Right's poster child for the evils of cancel culture. "I learned that what was happening to me had a name," Sandmann said in his remarks[2] at the convention. "It was called 'being canceled.' As in annulled. As in revoked. As in made void. Canceled is what's happening to people around this country who refuse to be silenced by the Far Left. Many are being fired, humiliated, or even threatened. And often, the media is a willing participant. But I would not be canceled." To further punctuate his rebellion, Sandmann ended his speech by placing a MAGA hat on his head.

In a world divorced from history and common sense, Sandmann's claims might have been plausible. Society is obsessed with enforcing binaries, and not only for gender norms. Everything must be black or white, wrong or right, Democrat versus Republican, good versus evil. The binary that conservatives are peddling is Far Left cancel culture versus conservative patriotism. Trump's rise to power—along with the rise of Trumpism—has only exacerbated the "us versus them" division in America. Yes, progressives are canceling people, places, and things, but despite their claims, conservatives and their rowdy affiliates have come up with their own version of cancel culture as well. In fact, canceling has become one of the defining characteristics of the conservative political party. Typically, the conservative takes on cancel culture are deployed to support societal norms, like patriarchy and white privilege. They frame themselves as the underdogs, fighting against the politically correct Left, when in fact they are the status quo. Conservatives love to defend loud bullies like Bill O'Reilly, Glenn Beck, Sean Hannity, Sarah Palin, and Ann Coulter. The cost of entry into conservative politics and their version of cancel culture is a hard stance against LGBTQIA rights, Black Lives Matter, abortion, and anything spoken out of the mouth of a Clinton, Obama, or Kennedy, along with isolationist politics, evangelical Christianity, and white supremacy.

Since the 1960s, conservatives have framed their cancel culture as either a moral crusade or one rooted in deep patriotism. Unlike progressives, who choose to cancel things based on social justice issues and human rights, conservatives are motivated to cancel based on their faith and self-proclaimed love of country. "What would Jesus do?" is the conservative motto, and American exceptionalism guides their agenda. Given the patriarchy embraced by their nationalism and their faith, it should come as no surprise that white cis-het men, who are leading the moral crusades that toe an evangelical Christian line, are at the center of conservative acts of cancel culture. You can take it all the way back to more than fifty-five years ago when conservative, evangelical Christians launched a full-fledged attack on the hit pop band the Beatles after John Lennon was quoted[3] as saying the band was "more popular than Jesus." Lennon tried to clarify his remarks in 1966. "I'm not saying that we're better, or greater, or comparing us with Jesus Christ as a person." But that was not good enough for the band's once-loyal Christian fans. At that time, most Americans were churchgoing Christians, with prayer being commonplace in public schools and large gatherings. Protestant Christianity was so mainstream in American society at the time that even identifying as a Catholic politician—as did former president John F. Kennedy Jr.—was the subject of national debate. Conservatives in the 1960s, sanctified by their nationalism and religiosity, were not about to let a foreign pop band critique their lord and savior without repercussions.

"The repercussions were big, especially in the Bible Belt," recalled bandmate George Harrison[4] in *The Beatles Anthology.* "In the South, they were having a field day."

"The backlash faced by the Beatles in the 1960s wasn't your average controversy," says Jon Pierre, a longtime music exec and member of the Recording Academy. "It was one of the first major examples of a distinctly American and Christian ideal that permeates Hollywood and U.S. media in a way that international audiences find perplexing. The purveyors of the British Invasion didn't do their research. America was God and country for the entirety of its short life, and the idea that the Fab Four foreigners were 'more popular than Jesus' was just too much for the parents of their screaming teenage daughters."

When a radio station in Birmingham, Alabama, gave their listeners an opportunity to send their Beatles records in so they could be fed into a wood chipper, the bold cancellation sparked a viral movement across the Bible Belt. The next thing you knew, countless bonfires were taking place across the Deep South, with former fans tossing their vinyl records into the flames. The matter even caught the attention of the Ku Klux Klan, who went so far as to nail Beatles records to a burning cross in retaliation for their comments. Despite the mounting tension, the world's most famous band simply chalked up the backlash to Americans' ignorance. But it's also important to note that just like their white male cis-het haters, they, too, were white and cis-het males—making their ability to recover from the controversy easier than it would have been for women, people of color, and LGBTQIA individuals. Later, we'll look at how other public figures, those without white, male, cis-het privilege, have less luck bouncing back from conservative cancel culture.

"I must admit we didn't really take it too seriously at all," bandmate Paul McCartney once told biographer Barry Miles. "We just thought, 'Yes, well, you can see what it is. It's hysterical, low-grade American thinking.'"

During this time, it was clear that religiosity and control—not democratic principle and/or social change—were inspiring these actions. The Beatles were so popular with the youth of America that they were able to pose a perceived threat to conservatives who were losing their grip on the younger generation.

Conservatives ultimately lost the culture wars of the late 1960s and 1970s because progressives and their icons dominated the airwaves and public consciousness during the countercultural movement. Legends such as Dr. Martin Luther King Jr., Harvey Milk, Gloria Steinem, and Angela Davis were cultural movers and shakers whose power didn't come from a political office. Conservatives were in desperate need of finding figures who could be their own media-friendly voices, people who could push their agenda faster than an elected official could in Congress.

One of the loudest voices of that era[5] came from staunch conservative Phyllis Schlafly, who was described by the ultraconservative Eagle Forum as the "most articulate and successful opponent of the radical feminist movement." During a time in which America was seeing feminism go mainstream, thanks to progressive women such as Gloria Steinem, Betty Friedan, bell hooks, Audre Lorde, and others, Schlafly led a crusade against women's rights. As feminists began to push for the Equal Rights Amendment, a law that would have ensured federal gender equality within the Constitution, Schlafly insisted that such a legislative change would destroy the rights and privileges of womanhood as she saw it. It was this fear that inspired her to create the STOP ERA movement, one of the fiercest oppositions to women's rights in American history. Unlike previous acts of sexism from male chauvinists, Schlafly provided an alternative to the battle of the sexes of the 1970s. She cleverly weaponized women to do the dirty deeds of opposing the women's rights movement.

STOP ERA is an acronym for *Stop Taking Our Privileges*—which Schlafly and her conservative female supporters argued were already protected under the laws of the time—combined with *Equal Rights Amendment.* Their robust campaign argued that by creating gender-neutral policies, women would be deprived of the very attributes that made them special. Ironically, similar rhetoric can now be heard within trans-exclusionary radical feminist (TERF) spaces that argue that transgender women being considered a part of the feminist movement negatively impacts the unique experiences of cisgender women. What made the STOP ERA movement different was that it was focused on building a coalition based on identity politics that went beyond gender alone. Major supporters were already members of Schlafly's conservative group, Eagle Forum, and were proud members of the Far Right side of the Republican Party. Like in most conservative movements, their Christian faith was essential to their demands against gender equality. To them, a woman's place in society wasn't to be out competing with men in the workforce but embracing dignified servitude in the household. Even though she earned her own salary, Schlafly believed that the ERA would eliminate Social Security benefits for widows and homemakers—something that would lead to the destruction of the nuclear family. Contrary to critiques of the STOP ERA movement, Schlafly believed that such ideals helped women rather than harmed them. But it should also be noted that this was coming from the perspective of a privileged, white, cisgender, heterosexual woman who was propelled by her religious beliefs. Such a very narrow lens of society best explains why she decided to oppose a cause that wanted to dismantle the system she was personally benefiting from.

After her ten-year fight, which included cross-country protesting, debating feminists in the media, hosting political rallies, lobbying conservative leaders, and writing polarizing literature, the ratification of the ERA fell three states short of the number needed to add it to the Constitution. Schlafly's efforts were successful; her anti-feminist movement would ensure that such a policy wouldn't pass even after her death in 2016. Today, the ERA has still not become the law of the land, and the push for its passing has waned. Was Phyllis Schlafly activating cancel culture? Through the lens of conservative cancel culture, she was. She saw a progressive world coming for the life she knew, the systems she benefited from. The fact that she was able to galvanize the Right around her cause shows how real the threat of feminism and progressives were to them. Schlafly may have thought her way of life was under attack, but her efforts helped—at least momentarily—shore up a system of male superiority that harmed women who didn't have the same privilege as she had.

The faith-based godfather of conservative cancel culture must be recognized as Jerry Falwell. Falwell, who passed away in 2007, was a longtime televangelist and conservative activist who used his Southern Baptist pastor's pulpit to condemn anything and everything he deemed unholy. Back then, he also helped fill conservative cancel culture's void of charismatic public figures who could influence the public nationwide. During the last decades of the twentieth century, Falwell took on progressive and countercultural institutions who were advancing LGBTQIA rights and sexual freedoms. In 1981, he sued adult-entertainment publication *Penthouse* for $10 million after they published an article that included an interview he did with freelancers, next to a photo of a *Penthouse* model. The courts rejected his complaint, just like they did during the controversial Supreme Court trial *Hustler Magazine v. Falwell,* where he battled another pornographic publication (that time for doing a parody on him).

Falwell framed his religious views as family values during a time when most Americans were more conservative in their social views. Separation between church and state, although stated in the Constitution, was not yet a political reality. Falwell, a spiritual leader, benefited from a society that promoted prayer in school and treated the Bible as the second American constitution. He thrived in making moral arguments against what he believed was the secular destruction of American values. Lauded by many political leaders, Falwell gained credibility in society as the voice of reason and faith for those who were more inclined to trust God over science, faith over politics. The iconic faith leader turned cancel culture into a modern-day religious crusade that tried to derail the separation between church and state.

In the latter half of the twentieth century, new groups were finding ways to call for conservative values to be upheld. Conservatives began to realize that progressive organizations like the NAACP, Urban League, ACLU, and Planned Parenthood were effective because they were able to lobby both the public at large and politicians. In response, America witnessed a rise in conservative groups dedicated to family values, morals, and confronting a liberal society. Since 1977, the American Family Association (AFA) has been one of the leading national conversative Christian groups geared toward advancing their religious fundamental beliefs. Labeled as an anti-LGBTQIA hate group by the Southern Poverty Law Center, the non-profit organization also stands against pornography and abortion. To put it bluntly, their sole mission is rooted in canceling anything that is LGBTQIA, "pornographic," or that promotes women's reproductive rights. For AFA, these issues are an affront to the patriarchal, nuclear family that they believe promotes traditional moral values. According to their messaging, same-sex couples are incapable of raising decent children, *Roe v. Wade* would forever destroy families, and any form of nudity in the media is a devious attempt to indoctrinate the minds of impressionable youth.

The AFA has two groups within its organization, the

One Million Moms and the One Million Dads projects, which are tasked with stopping the alleged "exploitation of children" by the media. Although they are named "one million," many groups, including GLAAD, have questioned those numbers, given their small social media following and engagement, which don't suggest anything close to those figures. Regardless of the actual size of their followings, these groups have found success in canceling progressive imagery on television. From national political issues to downright petty media observations, there is no cause too small or large for the AFA to mobilize behind.

By the late 1980s / early 1990s, there was a new form of cancel culture on the block: political correctness. Political correctness started in academia as an effort to avoid offense or disadvantage to marginalized members of society. The Right quickly grabbed hold of the term and turned it into an insult. As they did with cancel culture, conservatives complained that political correctness was the enemy of free speech. All this effort at not offending people was a real cramp in their style. High-profile scholar Allan Bloom published[6] his bestselling book *The Closing of the American Mind* in 1987 and stoked fear that political correctness was a danger to higher education. Dinesh D'Souza took things[7] even further with his book *Illiberal Education: The Politics of Sex and Race on Campus,* complaining about multiculturalism, affirmative action, and the evolution of curricula (known as *canon busting*). When many colleges began promoting a culture around sexual consent with the "No Means No" campaign, it was roundly ridiculed by everyone from standup comics to the mainstream news. But just like with criticism of cancel culture, slinging the term *PC* was a slippery way to avoid substantive discussion about important issues like race, gender, homophobia, or misogyny. When Antioch College in Illinois established an affirmative sexual consent rule for students in the 1990s, it was met with both horror and ridicule. Late-night comics groaned that no one would ever have college sex again. It was mocked as ridiculous that anyone should have to get consent before getting intimate. From a contemporary vantage point, where consent is taught to preschoolers, it's a good reminder that what seems far-fetched now can often end up being an accepted practice. And the awareness around diversity that political correctness was meant to highlight did not, in the end, kill free speech.

In the last ten years, conservative politicians have all but given up on selling a platform of ideas and initiatives to Americans and have embraced a sort of schoolyard bully's attitude toward anything remotely modern. As America has evolved and become more diverse and more accepting of progressive values, conservatives have retreated to whining about these changes on cable television rather than putting forth a real agenda, which is why they're now losing the culture wars. It's not rocket science; it's common sense. Of course the fight for civil rights was going to overrule white supremacy in national legislation. Advancements for women, LGBTQIA people, and people of color meant an end to a lot of the tolerated discrimination that defined America pre-1960s. Conservative cancel culture has been a counterargument to the progressiveness that has emerged. Since then, conservatives have continued to shoot themselves in the foot by standing by their racism at the expense of losing their moral and patriotic identity.

At the turn of the century, conservative cancel culture danced on the line between importance and frivolousness in a way that backfired in the public eye. As his popularity had begun to fade, evangelical leader Jerry Falwell decided to take his anti-LGBTQIA efforts to newer and more bizarre heights. In 1999, he called for families to boycott the hit children's program *Teletubbies*. Tinky Winky, one of the brightly colored characters that had screens on their bellies, was accused of being a gay symbol. Falwell came to this conclusion because Tinky Winky was purple, a gay-pride color, had a triangular antenna, often a queer symbol, and sometimes carried a purse. Under the headline "Parents Alert: Tinky Winky Comes Out of the Closet," an article published in Falwell's very own *National Liberty Journal*[8] bizarrely claimed that Tinky Winky had the voice of a young boy.

Falwell took to the press, condemning the show and remarking that "role modeling the gay lifestyle is damaging to the moral lives of children." The controversy quickly backfired, with those affiliated with the show calling Falwell's remarks outlandish. "The fact that he carries a magic bag doesn't make him gay," Steve Rice, a spokesman for Itsy Bitsy Entertainment Co., which licenses *Teletubbies* in the United States, told CBS News at the time.[9] "It's a children's show, folks. To think we would be putting sexual innuendo in a children's show is kind of outlandish."

"Who's Falwell going to out next, Winnie the Pooh? Or maybe, Barney; he's purple, you know," said Barry Lynn, executive director of Americans United for Separation of Church and State, in a 1999 press release from the organization. "If Falwell and his fundamentalist friends had their way," Lynn concluded, "there'd be nothing on the tube but TV preachers and the weather channel. I'd rather watch the 'Teletubbies' than televangelists."

"Jerry Falwell's paranoia about gay people has reached a new and ludicrous high-water mark," said David Smith, a spokesman for the Human Rights Campaign, during the debacle. "As farcical as it may sound, Falwell's latest ranting has serious consequences."

While the use of pornography, explicit music lyrics, and violence in media was still deemed a worthwhile moral public debate—trying to find homosexuality within a non-sexual children's character just seemed laughable. It became clear that Falwell had taken his religiosity to levels[10] that were beyond the fair concern for social welfare, and just a cheap attempt to attack the Left. At this point, he became just another angry, white, cis-het man ranting at things he found problematic.

Conservatives were still being driven by faith and patriotism, but as most Americans became less religious, faith-based appeals to cancel were less effective. As the U.S. became more diverse and all manner of inclusivity became policy and law, those old-school Christian values had to share space with other religions and ways of life. While many Americans embraced this new, diverse reality, conservatives doubled down. To use a word they love, conservatives were *triggered* by any kind of forward motion. At the top of the contemporary conservatives' trigger list is Christmas. It seems they'd rather have coal in their stockings than accept that anyone might celebrate Christmas in a nontraditional way or not celebrate Christmas at all. Aisha Harris's article for *Slate,* titled "Santa Shouldn't Be a White Man Anymore; It's Time to Give St. Nick His Long Overdue Makeover," got the ball rolling. Megyn Kelly, then a star on Fox News, took to the airways to console American children that, not to worry, "Santa is what he is. Which is white." She went on to say that just because something makes you uncomfortable doesn't mean it has to change. How dare a Black woman reimagine a mystical, fictional character!

The next nail in the Christmas coffin, according to conservatives, was the Starbucks holiday cup. Fans of the coffee giant have always looked forward to the holiday cup, which changes each year and has sported snowmen, snowflakes, and various Christmas ornaments. In the winter of 2015, the company decided to remove explicitly Christmas-themed designs on the holiday cups and released them in a simple red. Starbucks stated that they wanted to create a cup with a more inclusive feeling that could be seen as a celebration of anyone's holiday. Seems simple enough. Far-right evangelical internet personality Joshua Feuerstein took to Facebook to cry, "Starbucks removed Christmas from their cups because they hate Jesus." He urged his followers to use the hashtag #MerryChristmasStarbucks and to ask baristas to write *Merry Christmas* on their coffee cups instead of their names. Donald Trump also weighed in[11] while on the campaign trail. "No more Merry Christmas at Starbucks. Maybe we should boycott Starbucks," he said. Noting that there was a Starbucks in the lobby of New York's Trump Tower, he added, "By the way, that's the end of that lease."

It's become predictable to see "the silent majority" of conservatives taking aggressive stances on anything from queer characters in Disney movies to Beyoncé music videos that contain pro-Black messages. Conservatives tried to cry cancel culture when, in 2021, toy company Hasbro changed the brand name of Mr. Potato Head to Potato Head. They were not altering the name of the characters within their toy line, but just the brand's name. So yes, a fan of Mr. or Mrs. Potato Head can still purchase those toys— they will just be inside a box branded Potato Head. But conservatives were quick to become reactionary, suggesting that progressives were to blame for canceling gender within the toy company.

"Look out, Mr. Potato Head, you're next," said Republican congressman Matt Gaetz during the 2021 Conservative Political Action Conference.[12] "I'm sorry, I think now he's going by Potato X. He can't be Mr. Potato." The congressman was acting as if cancel culture had reared its ugly head, citing other false examples of cancellations that didn't exist, such as claiming that the Walt Disney Company "canceled its own founder," Walt Disney. In fact, in 2019, Disney added content warnings to the beginning of some of their classics, such as *Peter Pan, Lady and the Tramp, The Jungle Book,* and others on their streaming platform Disney+, explaining that these films contained "negative depictions of and/or mistreatments of cultures or peoples." These stereotypes were wrong then and are wrong now. In the case of Hasbro, one could argue that *if* progressives had protested the toy company based on gender and inclusion, there might be some gravitas to Gaetz's rant. Unfortunately for him, no such protest had been made. Still, he seemed to be infatuated with the versatility of the toy—making even more outrageous assertions that would seem unimaginable until he opened his mouth.

"See, to me the whole concept of the Mr. Potato Head was you could move the parts around," Gaetz argued before a crowd of hundreds. "Mr. Potato Head was America's first transgender doll and even he got canceled."

Seriously? It's idiotic at best—and intentionally misleading at worst—to suggest that gender-neutral toys are transgender by default or that they have never existed. Teddy bears, perhaps one of the most gender-neutral toys of all time, were around long before people were playing with Mr. Potato Head in the 1950s. But that wasn't the point Gaetz was trying to make—he was simply invested in reframing cancel culture as a mass hysteria, progressives ruining the conformity to the family values of his political party. How ironic that in March 2021, reports would claim that the Department of Justice was investigating Gaetz for engaging in sex trafficking[13] and an alleged sexual relationship with a seventeen-year-old. Perhaps the staunch conservative who was worrying so much about the future of America's moral compass should have been more worried about his own.

It's a sense of entitlement that drives the conservatives' decision to cancel the way that they do. Conservatism may be rooted in Christianity, but it is driven by a desire to retain power. And conservatives lean on faulty interpretations of American rights to justify their behavior. Which begs the question: Are the Constitution and God's law one and the same? Ask media personalities like Sean Hannity or the now disgraced Bill O'Reilly and they would argue that this country was founded on Christian values. *In God We Trust* is scripted on national landmarks, and many insist that you shouldn't remove the word *God* from the Pledge of Allegiance. But the framers of the Constitution clearly recognized from the jump that this was to be a country that also included and protected people of various faiths, which is why freedom of religion is in the Bill of Rights. Also, morality isn't only defined by Christianity, and to think so is an act of religious bigotry.

Long before politicians like Matt Gaetz were belly-aching about how toys were being canceled, conservatives were looking for ways to shift actual policy. Until the early 1980s, the movement was taking place on a grassroots level—from the church to the streets. What was missing was the backing of legislators, conservative elected officials who could validate their collective outrage. The addition of political power to this faith-based canceling was the fuel the movement needed, because where else could they get such power? Society was quickly becoming more progressive as the culture wars were advancing rights for marginalized communities. By the 1970s, racial civil rights, a woman's right to choose, LGBTQIA liberation, and a new wave of feminism captured the hearts and minds of a nation that was once antagonistic to such changes. Those who were on the Far Right appeared to be out of touch with what was becoming a more modern America. Unlike liberals, conservatives couldn't lean on pop culture figures and young protesters to drive their campaigns. Certainly, neither Falwell nor Schlafly held an appeal to the youth of that time. It would take a savvy politician to see the potential in joining forces with the religious right. And that savvy politician was Ronald Reagan.

"The rise of the religious right as a political force would prove a boon for Ronald Reagan, who in turn offered a reciprocal and lasting boost to the religious conservatives' political fortunes," religious scholar and theologist Dr. Anthea Butler said in a 2019 op-ed for CNN.[14] "In a campaign address on religious liberty, Reagan would indicate his support for the Moral Majority and evangelicals by saying, 'You can't endorse me, but I can endorse you.'"

The Reagan era gave conservatives a new opportunity to feel emboldened to cancel in a way that not only advanced their agenda but legitimized it. While the phrase is now firmly associated with Donald Trump, it was Reagan who, in 1980,[15] first boldly declared during his first presidential campaign: "Let's make America great again." He promised conservatives a revival of the old-fashioned Christian values that began to erode in the late 1960s. During Reagan's reign, conservatives fought in the courts and pushed regressive policies. This was a different level of cancel culture for conservatives that was more than just public rants—it was actions that made an impact. Reagan succeeded in empowering the conservative ethos that restoring America meant a return to moral values— weaponizing church and state as forces to cancel progressive ideals.

One of Reagan's first cancellation campaigns was the

war on drugs. Richard Nixon may have initiated the war on drugs, but Reagan is more closely associated with it for the legislation he established. Addressing illegal drug use had historically been handled with a public health approach, but with a sharp turn to the right, Reagan made it a criminal issue. Hyping up the dangers of drugs, Reagan declared that drugs posed an existential threat to national security.

On the face of it, Reagan was trying to cancel drug use, but this cancellation had more far-reaching consequences. The spread of recreational drugs in American culture in the 1970s was driven by disco, hippies, and trafficking in major urban cities. Conservatives argued that the progressive ideals of the countercultural movement during this time were responsible for the moral decay of America. Many religious leaders of the 1980s blamed sex, drugs, and rock and roll as being responsible for the social crisis they were now experiencing due to the rise of AIDS and the crack epidemic. Rather than embrace these challenges and attempt to improve them, conservatives chose to demonize the victims of these epidemics.

Even though white Americans were using drugs at a similar rate to Black and Brown Americans, the war on drugs' focus on crack rather than powder cocaine meant that far more Black and Brown people were imprisoned. By the mid-1980s, there was a five-year minimum sentence for possession of five grams of crack cocaine—a sentence you'd need to possess five hundred grams of powder cocaine to receive. Powder cocaine was an expensive drug, used mostly by affluent white people, while cheaper crack cocaine was used by poorer people and people of color. The crack use of that time did not receive the kind of care, empathy, and attention that the more recent opioid crisis receives. The number of losses due to opioids has caused us to rethink how we collectively empathize with those impacted by addiction. We know now that addiction is a complex disease that no one chooses. That wasn't the case back in the day during the rise of crack cocaine. Countless Black and Brown people were dismissed as irresponsible, reckless, and criminal as they struggled with substance abuse. Reagan's national war on drugs criminalized addiction and mental health problems. In Reagan's time as president, the FBI's budget for drug enforcement increased from eight million to ninety-five million, with a particular focus on crack. It led to stricter jail sentences, which disproportionately targeted people of color. Along with canceling a certain kind of drug use, conservatives were canceling the potential of hundreds of thousands of people of color. Much has been written on this complicated history, and I recommend *The New Jim Crow* by Michelle Alexander,[16] *Locking Up Our Own* by James Forman Jr.,[17] and *The First Civil Right* by Naomi Murakawa[18] for those who'd like to learn more.

Reagan's war on drugs couldn't have been as effective if it had only been fueled by legislation. To pull it off, he needed public buy-in. And that's where his wife, Nancy Reagan, came in. During a visit to an elementary school in Oakland, California, First Lady Nancy Reagan was asked by a schoolgirl what she should do if offered drugs. This was a turning point: The First Lady could have offered her a nuanced response that provided more explanation about the dangers of drugs and empathy for a child who finds herself in a world where she could be offered drugs. But instead, she gave this child a three-word mantra: *Just say no*. It was 1982, and the First Lady was telling every youth across America to "Just Say No" to drugs at a time when the war on drugs was being escalated by her husband's policies. Nancy's backing of an antidrug campaign would lead to a concerted effort to scare youth from drug use, but also to imply that keeping away from drugs was a simple, individual choice. With her logic, if you were on drugs, you had said yes to them and therefore you were personally responsible for whatever hardship came your way as a result. The First Lady relied on moral appeals to persuade those around her to spread fear without considering nuance, facts, or compassion. "Just Say No" was about making those suffering from drug addiction the scapegoats of a failed criminal justice system. And it did not come with the tools people needed to reverse their circumstances.

African American studies scholar Marc Lamont Hill, who grew up under the "Just Say No" antidrug campaign, recalls that his first memory of Nancy Reagan was watching her special guest appearance on a 1983 episode of the hit sitcom *Diff'rent Strokes*. In the episode, Reagan warns a classroom of diverse young schoolchildren to avoid drugs around them. Hill took issue with the fact that "Just Say No" emphasizes the word *just,* as if it's that simple for people who live in environments where the presence of drugs is pervasive. "I think Nancy Reagan was well-intentioned, but ultimately became an unknowing pitchwoman for a vicious, draconian drug war," said Hill to *The Washington Post*[19] following the former First Lady's death in 2016. "They didn't appreciate the relationship between drug abuse and public health, mental illness, resources, jobs, et cetera, so part of what the Reagan administration did is individualize a collective problem."

Nancy Reagan's role in the war on drugs cannot be overstated. Her "Just Say No" campaign convinced millions of Americans to hate drugs and the people who used them. It encouraged a lack of empathy for those struggling with addiction and encouraged support for policies that further criminalized them. What was initially a cancellation of drugs morphed into a cancellation of empathy. Mass incarceration wouldn't be possible without the cultural approval of locking people up for either minor drug charges or health issues like addiction. The First Lady's achievements proved how political cancel culture was much more powerful than boycotts or protests on the conservative side. Unlike previous grassroots conservative movements, this form of cancel culture was coming straight from the White House.

"Casual drug users should be taken out and shot," said Los Angeles police chief Daryl Gates during a Senate hearing[20] on drugs in 1990. This was nearly a decade after Reagan's campaign had taken off, and now Gates was ready to further demonize drug use. Gates would become the founder of the infamous DARE (Drug Abuse Resistance Education) program, which immediately took off nationwide despite the lack of evidence about its effectiveness. It actually became apparent very quickly that kids who took part in the program were as likely to do drugs as kids who did not. And yet, for a time, DARE was in 75 percent of U.S. schools. America would have never ended up with such problematic programs as DARE had it not been for Nancy Reagan pushing "Just Say No."

There wouldn't have been the ruthless "three strikes" policy under the now-infamous Crime Bill of 1994 of the Clinton administration without the "Just Say No" campaign of the 1980s. The three-strikes laws were implemented in different ways in different states. In some states, a third serious offense (murder, rape, aggravated assault) means an automatic life sentence. But in states like California, the third strike can be robbery or drug possession.

If Reagan was an example of a politician moving toward prominent Christians in order to shore up his power, the era of Donald Trump displayed the reverse. Still paying lip service to traditional values of church and family—rejecting progressive change that would undermine those stated values—conservatives began accepting Faustian bargains with all manner of extremists in order to shore up their power. No one understood this willingness better than Donald Trump.

"In the past, candidates' performances of Christianity have been strong points for voters, but Trump's ascendancy with evangelicals has eviscerated that expectation," said Anthea Butler in a 2016 op-ed[21] for *The Guardian*. "Evangelicals, like other voters, can be very pragmatic about the issues they want addressed by the leadership they support." Historically, to succeed in American politics—particularly as a Republican—candidates had to at least make a show of their faith. Attend Sunday services, join in prayer circles, take meetings with church leaders. But to Butler's point, Trump simply opted out of this game. No one believed a word when he pretended to not be able to discuss the Bible in an interview with Bloomberg News because his relationship to it was "so special." But Evangelicals were willing to play along with this charade to get a conservative, antichoice president. In fact, turning a blind eye to Trump's faux Christianity allowed them to further their own cancellation goals.

"Moral issues once drove white evangelical votes but, first when Obama was elected and then when the Supreme Court struck down the federal ban on same-sex marriage in June of 2015, what remained was their fear," said Butler in a 2019 op-ed for NBC News.[22] "Trump promised justices a return to a time when they felt less fear, and he delivered, at least on the former. White evangelical fealty to him is firm. Evangelicals in America are not simply a religious group; they are a political group inexorably linked to the Republican Party."

"When Trump used the term 'American carnage' in his inaugural address, evangelicals listened; they, too, believed America is in decline," continued Butler, who also wrote the 2021 book[23] *White Evangelical Racism: The Politics of Morality in America.* "Their imagined powerlessness, and the need for a strong authoritarian leader to protect them, is at the root of their racial and social animus. Their persecution complex is a heady mix of their fear of socialists, Muslims, independent women, LGBT people and immigration. Their feelings of fragility, despite positions of power, make them vote for people like Donald Trump— and morally suspect candidates like Roy Moore. Rhetoric, not morality, drives their voting habits."

From the moment of his grand announcement that he was running for president, Trump's language was mired in racism, bigotry, and his own brand of cancel culture, which appealed directly to this evangelical base. "When Mexico sends its people, they're not sending their best," Trump said on that day in June 2015.[24] "They're bringing drugs. They're bringing crime. They're rapists. And some, I assume, are good people."

Univision, partaking in their own cancel culture, decided to no longer air the Miss USA pageant and severed ties with Trump's co-owned Miss Universe Organization in response to Trump's racist comments about Mexican immigrants. Trump, along with his supporters, joined in on social media to berate the Spanish-language media company for what they considered to be a form of political correctness and called on the public to boycott them. Using the PC label was a way of distracting from the value-based position Univision was taking on Trump's racist remarks.

Similar talk from his supporters also made headlines when major retail company Macy's decided to drop Trump's menswear fashion line from all their department stores following his offensive remarks. "Macy's is a company that stands for diversity and inclusion," the company said in a statement at the time. "We are disappointed and distressed by recent remarks about immigrants from Mexico . . . who have made so many valuable contributions to the success of our nation." Trump called on his supporters to boycott Macy's, while insisting that he had pulled his products from the department store, rather than him being dumped by them.

In these instances, one could suggest that conservatives were only retaliating against the liberal stances of these companies. This cause-and-effect approach has been used to frame liberals as antagonists and conservatives as defenders of their individual freedoms. One of the current right-wing media narratives is that the Right is being provoked by progressives who want to push their ideologies upon them. Of course, this isn't the case. Progressives have an agenda of expanding rights for more people. While it claims to be upholding traditional values, the new right-wing version of cancel culture is primarily rooted in an obsession with reinforcing traditional power structures. Whether they're reinforcing values or power, it's always at the expense of diversity. In other words, reinforcing white supremacy. Progressives may cancel a brand for criticizing citizens who protest the American flag. Conservatives would rally around that brand for defending a symbol they hold dear.

It's undeniable that the rise of Trumpism and the MAGA spirit speaks to most conservatives, though some may bristle at the movement's less dignified tendencies. To "Make America Great Again" is to return it to the culture and thinking that gave conservatives the confidence and power they grew accustomed to. Turn on any major right-wing program, and it's not hard to spot when and why they cancel the way that they do. Imagine living in a country as a straight white Christian male who has benefited from decades of racial, gender, and sexuality discrimination, and suddenly, it all starts to come crashing down.

The history of this kind of privilege is so old many conservatives believe it's the natural state of things. "White conservatives used brute force to enslave the Indigenous

people's bodies when they intruded upon Africa in the
sixteenth and seventeenth centuries, they used Eurocen-
tric Christianity to enslave the people's minds in the name
of white patriarchal supremacy," civil rights attorney and
activist Michael Coard argues. "That expanded into the
widespread and systemic use of Christian missionaries.
Fast-forward to now, and that same white patriarchal
Christian supremacy exists. And it's promoted by white
men and their brainwashed acolytes to cancel and subju-
gate people of color and progressive views." The victories
progressives have won in advancing civil rights for everyone who doesn't fall within this Christian, heteronormative, Anglo-Saxon, patriarchal umbrella have driven
conservatives to cancel even more.

There is a clear link between the hate of Trump's rhetoric and the ways in which conservatives chose to cancel
during his presidency. In many cases, Trump's brash de-
meanor emboldened the way conservatives were canceling things they didn't agree with. Trumpism ushered in a
new wave of conservative cancel culture that led to more
divisive and destructive methods for right-wingers to use
against the progressive politics that had grown popular
in the previous decade. Just a few examples of Trump-
led cancellations include opting out of the Paris Climate
Agreement, gutting the State Department, revoking a
rule that protected funding for Planned Parenthood, and
failed attempts to cancel Obamacare. This new tone con-
trasted with the days of great friendships between peo-

ple of opposing parties. President Joe Biden has spoken often of his close friendship with the late conservative congressman John McCain. These days, the rhetoric is so divisive that longtime Black political operative Randy Robinson, a conservative, is now concerned about being affiliated with the GOP due to Trump's influence.

"The conservative movement is in crisis," says Robinson, who has historically campaigned for Republicans before Trump's takeover in battleground states, such as Pennsylvania. "It has allowed the GOP to manipulate its principles for the sake of political power due to Trump's impact." Robinson, who did not vote for Trump in either of his presidential elections, believes that "conservatism is the most powerful political philosophy for governing within a democracy due to its stability and consistency. However, because of its leaning on the Republican Party and its vocal population of racist, nativist, nationalist ties, conservatism wears the black eye for being so closely associated." Even this true believer can't get on board with how his party has been warped.

If conservatives were interested in gaining popularity the rational way, by representing everyone in America, they would try to reflect that America in their party—but they're not. Apart from Candace Owens, a millennial Black conservative who has maintained a large following for her Far Right rhetoric, there are not many fresh, diverse faces within the movement. The demographics of America are most certainly not in conservatives' favor. As I mentioned at the end of the previous chapter, if current trends continue, by 2050, most Americans will be non-white. Rather than embrace demographic realities, contemporary conservatives have allowed "us and them" to blossom. Those who supported Trump's 2017 Muslim travel ban were invested in the cancellation of foreigners whom they perceived as a threat. Others who supported building a wall on the Mexican border to block immigrants made it clear that they wanted to cancel the immigration of diverse individuals coming into the country. Several studies debunk the myths, such as those exposed in the Cato Institute's 2021 report *The Most Common Arguments Against Immigration and Why They're Wrong,* that immigrants (legal and undocumented) abuse welfare and commit more crimes than American-born citizens, but that hasn't stood in the way of the commonly held conservative belief that immigration is bad for America.

Given their lack of interest in a steadily diversifying population, conservatives have taken another route to maintain power—messing with elections. Whether it's through gerrymandering, restricting voting locations, or simply denying the results of conservative losses, the conservative party has become the anti-vote party. Fortified by Trump's authoritarian rhetoric, many in the Republican base have bought into the lie that any election where a Democrat wins must be rigged. Conservatives are willing to cancel democracy to try to retain a grasp on power.

America has had a long history with voter suppression, starting with its creation when only white landowning men could vote. Even as more and more groups of people were eligible to vote, barriers were put in place to make it next to impossible. Poll taxes, literacy tests, and English-language requirements were all meant to discourage Black, immigrant, and low-income populations. Following the televised, brutal beatings of peaceful protesters at Selma, Alabama, Lyndon Johnson signed the Voting Rights Act into law in 1965. Under the guise of it no longer being necessary, the Supreme Court gutted the Voting Rights Act in their 2013 *Shelby County v. Holder* decision. In the absence of federal oversight, many red states have taken the opportunity to make voting more and more difficult— for some people. Conservatives in states like Texas, Georgia, and Florida discourage voting by purging voter rolls, cutting down on early voting, making ID requirements stricter, removing voting stations, and forcing people to have to travel great distances to vote, among other tactics. By creating unreasonable challenges to voting, claiming they are necessary to avoid nonexistent voter fraud, conservatives have decided that if they can't beat them, then just cheat them.

The anti-democratic nature of conservatives' effort at voter suppression is troubling enough, but what's more dire is the embrace of brutality. One of the early signs of the modern Far Right's shameless crusade to threaten violence in public came in 2015 from RedState.com editor

Erick Erickson. Erickson, also a popular talk-radio host at the time, was angered by a *New York Times* editorial calling for gun control after the tragic San Bernardino mass shooting. To make his point, Erickson shot seven bullet holes[25] in the paper, took a picture of it, and posted it to Twitter. He encouraged his followers to do the same. The situation generated online discussions about free speech, gun violence, and conservatives being noticeably hostile when challenged on policy issues. Erickson was calling for the cancellation of a free press when he didn't agree with its contents. Remember, this was just over a year before Trump started railing against "fake news." The only irony is that Erickson would later delete the post, become an anti-Trump conservative, and find himself as an op-ed contributor for the very same *New York Times* he shot up with seven rounds.

As I touched upon, in the summer of 2017, the country was shaken by the violent events that took place in Charlottesville, Virginia. Several Far Right groups descended on Charlottesville to protest the removal of confederate statues (which had been removed after the Charleston church shooting by a white supremacist, which killed nine Black church members, including their minister, in 2015). Neo-Nazis, neo-confederates, and Klansmen, among others, clashed with counter-protesters and the riot resulted in one dead and many injured. Many were stunned to see images of young white men holding burning torches and chanting, "Jews will not replace us!" and it's easy enough to discount this group of deplorables as a few too many bad apples, marching for various reasons and united by hate. What distinguished this riot from other acts of domestic terrorism was the response from the White House. Rather than give a predictable condemnation of white supremacy, then president Trump seemed to be sending a message to the fascists when he remarked that there were "very fine people on both sides." And if it wasn't his intention, that's the way his supporters took it. Just days after the rally, KKK grand wizard David Duke tweeted:[26] "Thank you President Trump for your honesty and courage in talking about Charlottesville & condemn the leftist terrorists BLM and Antifa." It used to be the case that Nazis and KKK members were reluctant to make themselves known, but why hide in the shadows when you think your president agrees with you?

Trump's response to the shooting at the Tree of Life Synagogue in Pittsburgh in 2018 was only marginally better. Robert Gregory Bowers entered the synagogue, which houses three separate congregations within its walls, and shot and killed eleven people and wounded six more. Bowers's attack was driven by anti-Semitism but also by anti-refugee animus. One of the synagogue's groups, Dor Hadash,[27] had participated in HIAS's (Hebrew Immigrant Aid Society) National Refugee Shabbat just a week earlier. Bowers had posted on the Far Right site Gab: "HIAS like to bring invaders in that kill our people. I can't watch as my people get slaughtered. Screw your optics, I'm going in."

While claiming that the violence was an anti-Semitic attack of "pure evil," Trump failed to acknowledge the anti-refugee sentiments that accompanied it. It's not surprising that he didn't want to speak out about anti-refugee rhetoric given how he was actively trying to cancel refugees in the U.S.

All conservatives—not only Trump—pretend that they want no part in cancel culture. They'd like to frame it as a tool of the Left, something frightening and un-American. A look at their behavior tells a different story. The fact is that conservatives embrace cancel culture wholeheartedly. In their version—one that longs for the days of their unrestricted power—they have tried canceling voting rights, immigration, the separation of church and state, gun safety laws, access to abortion, and the existence of transgendered people, to name a few. These are issues that the plurality of Americans support. Their attempts to do away with rights—such as the right to vote or abortion rights—represent enormous potential harm to countless people, and we ignore them at our peril. Conservatives hide their agenda[28] behind the veil of tradition, but tradition for them means a lesser piece of the American pie for too many to allow that lie to stand.

NOT ALL CANCELLATIONS
ARE THE SAME

Status—as defined by race, gender, class, and
social status—is often the deciding factor for
who gets canceled and who does not.

On May 12, 2021, Republican congressperson Liz Cheney was canceled by her own party. In an unprecedented turn of events, House Republicans officially removed Cheney, the daughter of former vice president Dick Cheney, from the number three position in the GOP conference. The reason: She wouldn't support her colleagues in pushing the "big lie" that claimed Donald Trump was cheated during the 2020 presidential election. In fact, Cheney, who has represented the state of Wyoming since 2017, doubled down on telling the public that Trump was lying and that there was no election fraud. Once passive on Trump's racist and incompetent leadership as someone who had previously voted for him, Cheney was one of the few from the Right in Congress who voted to impeach the former president for wrongdoing in the January 6 insurrection (his second impeachment trial).

"We cannot both embrace the big lie and embrace the Constitution," Cheney told the press[1] following the vote to remove her from power. "I will do everything I can to ensure that the former president never again gets anywhere near the Oval Office."

Among conservatives, there was debate about whether Cheney had been canceled or not. Some, like Republican congressman Ken Buck of Colorado, supported Cheney.[2] "Liz didn't agree with President Trump's narrative, and she was canceled," he told reporters following the vote. Others, like Sean Hannity of Fox News, did not. "Congresswoman Liz Cheney was booted from her GOP leadership position after months of nonstop negative remarks about Trump and those who support him," Hannity argued on his controversial,[3] right-wing prime-time show. "Now the media mob and Democrats are treating the congresswoman like she is some modern-day martyr. She is not."

What Cheney would learn is that cancel culture is a complicated business, and the way a cancellation lands is affected by your race, your gender, your politics, and ultimately, your status in the world. All cancellations are not equal—where you start in the world has an enormous impact on how they play out.

The irony of Cheney's situation is that as she was trying to cancel Trump, her party chose to cancel her instead. Cheney was over Trump because she believed his divisive politics had gone too far and led to a deadly insurrection that sought to ravage democracy. But conservatives recognized that despite national criticism, Trump remained a more influential figure within the party and that his power was unmatched. If the Republican Party had plans to take back the House of Representatives during the upcoming midterms, they would need his sway and money to help make it so. The GOP didn't care whether Cheney was wrong or right; they had bigger fish to fry. For them, criticizing the former president would only embolden the progressives they'd fought so hard to challenge over the years. What Liz Cheney was doing was blasphemous to what Republicans typically stand for. Unlike progressives, they don't cancel their own—unless they view someone committing an act of betrayal against the party.

"Having heard from so many of you in recent days, it's clear that we need to make a change," wrote congressional minority leader Kevin McCarthy in a letter regarding Cheney[4] days before her removal. "As such, you should anticipate a vote on recalling the Conference Chair this Wednesday."

Cheney's cancellation was an attempt by Republican leadership to make an example out of her for anyone else considering such a dissent. This was their bold play to unify and mobilize the party ahead of the midterm elections, to maintain power. In his letter, McCarthy, who's made himself one of Trump's most loyal political allies, argued that Cheney was "relitigating the past"—even though she was simply responding to Trump's false version of the election results. But McCarthy didn't care.

His job as top Republican in the House was to shift the party's focus and criticism toward the Democratic Party. Nonetheless, McCarthy's letter defined the GOP as being a "big tent party" of "free thought and debate" even though he was calling for the cancellation of a conference chair who criticized Trump.

Meanwhile, Trump vowed to fully back[5] a primary challenger against Cheney during her reelection and issued a no-holds-barred statement praising the House vote and teasing that he looked forward "to soon watching her as a Paid Contributor on CNN or MSDNC!" (combining MSNBC with DNC). He went on to say, "Liz Cheney is a bitter, horrible human being. I watched her yesterday and realized how bad she is for the Republican Party."

This political controversy—with all its ironies, hypocrisies, and utter madness—is a textbook example of how cancel culture isn't evenly, or equally, waged. Despite all his problematic and harmful ways, Donald Trump was never rejected by his own party in the same way Liz Cheney was. The conservatives' logic behind canceling Cheney was that they saw her beef with Trump as a distraction to the party's work to win reelection. Trump is so protected by Republicans that Cheney's departure from leadership was caused by the very polarizing power he projects and the fear he inspires. Cheney believes that her colleagues didn't vote to impeach him not because he was innocent but because they "were afraid for their own security."

"If you look at the vote to impeach, for example, there were members who told me that they were afraid for their own security—afraid, in some instances, for their lives," Cheney said during a May 2021 interview[6] with CNN host Jake Tapper on *The Lead*. "And that tells you something about where we are as a country, that members of Congress aren't able to cast votes, or feel that they can't, because of their own security."

Fear can often be at the heart of who gets canceled and how, and power remains a critical aspect in how people make decisions. Although modern cancel culture makes it easier for anyone to speak their mind, it's only natural that someone with limited power will think twice before taking on someone with more status. Who has status and who doesn't have status is, unfortunately, determined by identity. And those who are marginalized have the most to lose. Even within the relatively high-status subset that is Congress, there are distinctions between players. Liz Cheney comes from a powerful conservative family, with deep connections to the GOP. In some ways, she has a lot of power. It's not presidential-level power, however. She's also a woman. Even Senator Mitt Romney, who has consistently criticized Trump, has never been as ostracized by his fellow Republicans in the same way Cheney has. Which is why it's important to be conscious of the dynamics of gender and perceived power within cancel culture.

"The ways cancel culture affects certain individuals depends largely on who their primary audience is," says Christen Mandracchia, Ph.D., a pop culture scholar and historian. "Trump's base is conservative, and, therefore, it is difficult to impossible to 'cancel' him based on liberal or progressive reasons—it would have to be on conservative reasons, and it would have to be something that a wide cross-section of conservatives could not accept—like when the Dixie Chicks got rejected by their conservative base during the Bush years. It's all about the base." Despite being kicked out of office and off Twitter, Trump remains a central figure in conservative politics. Conservatives have not yet found that definitive reason to cancel him once and for all.

What happened to the iconic country music group the Chicks, formerly known as the Dixie Chicks, is an important example of the consequences that can occur when someone goes against the beliefs of their audience. During the height of the war on terrorism, the group performed in London, just days before the 2003 invasion of Iraq. While onstage at the Shepherd's Bush Empire theater, lead singer Natalie Maines told the crowd:[7] "Just so you know, we're on the good side with y'all. We do not want this war, this violence, and we're ashamed that the president of the United States is from Texas."

For an all-female, American group in one of the most

conservative music genres to speak out against their commander in chief, George W. Bush, while performing overseas, felt blasphemous to many. The timing couldn't have been any worse, and the optics set the Chicks up to be targets of sexist, hateful, and life-threatening attacks. This is a contrast from what happened to the Beatles, who mocked Christianity in the 1960s, and it should come as no surprise why: The Chicks were American women with progressive views in a conservative music genre, not male British pop stars being cheeky. The group members were labeled as traitors, and Maines was particularly singled out. Thousands of country radio stations blacklisted their music, and some of the DJs who still played them during that time were suspended. Conservative protesters could be seen on local and national news outlets destroying their Dixie Chicks CDs. The Kansas City station WDAF-AM went as far as to invite listeners to toss the group's records in trash cans they had outside their office as part of a nationwide boycott. Unlike the temporary backlash that the Beatles faced, the campaign against the Chicks was sustained. They were subjected to death threats and labeled as "Saddam's Angels" and "Dixie Sluts" by protesters who found them unpatriotic and not supportive of American troops in combat.

"The Chicks were the down-home, blond-haired bombshells next door that the Nashville establishment uplifted as pinups of conservatism—the perfect crossover stars," says Jon Pierre, who started his career executive producing country music albums in Nashville. "They were a commercial juggernaut in the same way Shania was, selling tens of millions of albums, but they never abandoned traditional country sounds and aesthetics in exchange for slickly produced pop and MTV-friendly marketing. Once they dipped their toes in the liberal waters of Bush-bashing, however, the betrayal was indelibly worse than any pop remix could ever be."

Conservative country star and rival of Maines at the time Toby Keith added fuel to the fire when he decided to project a doctored image of Maines cuddling with Iraqi dictator Saddam Hussein on a large screen at several of his concerts while she was being attacked in the press. But there were others at the time who questioned the cancellation the Dixie Chicks were facing. Although industry support for the music group wasn't equal to the backlash, there were those who questioned the use of patriotism in boycotting them altogether.

"They've cut such an honest groove with their career," said country legend Merle Haggard about the Chicks[8] to *Rolling Stone* at the time. "Because they don't like George Bush, should we take their records off? I really found that sort of scary. Are we afraid of criticism? And if so, why? It seems to me, we're guilty in this country of doing everything we've always opposed all my life. I'm almost afraid to say something. It got to the point where my wife said, 'Be careful what you say.' Well, that's really not the America I'm used to."

As I've highlighted previously, it's not only that the Chicks had voiced opinions their conservative fans didn't like but also that they did it while being female. In the tricky equation of cancel culture, a lack of patriotism from women outweighs free speech. If women or people of color don't toe the patriotic line, the pushback is particularly vicious. The fight surrounding free speech is essentially why tensions were extremely high when the Chicks decided to speak out against President Bush's decision to go to war with Iraq. Conservatives who were already in support of the Republican leader, a proud Texan, made the country trio scapegoats in a smear campaign that was more about building national support for the war than engaging in an actual debate. As a result, the controversy forced the Chicks into a sudden hiatus, as their once stellar records sales, sold-out tours, and nationwide acclaim took a massive hit. The controversy lasted for over a decade, until they finally released their follow-up album, *Gaslighter,* in 2020, fourteen years later.

To understand the role of gender and status when it comes to cancel culture, we can also look to the example of male country singer Morgan Wallen.[9] Hardship and career setback was not the plotline in his story when a video surfaced in January 2021, showing Wallen using the N-word. In the video, first released by TMZ, he tells a friend, "Take care of this nigger," referring to another person he was with in the footage.

In a statement Wallen released at the time, he said,

"I used an unacceptable and inappropriate racial slur that I wish I could take back. There are no excuses to use this type of language, ever. I want to sincerely apologize for using the word. I promise to do better."

Initially, the predictable cancellation quickly followed: Country radio stations cut Wallen's songs, streaming services dropped him from official playlists, his booking agent stopped working with him, and his label, Big Loud Records, suspended his recording contract. Even the Academy of Country Music—the Oscars of the genre—deemed him ineligible for the 2021 ACM Awards. Although he was a finalist due to his record sales, even the Billboard Music Awards disinvited him from appearing during their live taping.

"Morgan Wallen is a finalist this year based on charting," a spokesperson for Dick Clark Productions told *Billboard* at the time. "As his recent conduct does not align with our core values, we will not be including him on the show in any capacity (performing, presenting, accepting). It is heartening and encouraging to hear that Morgan is taking steps in his anti-racist journey and starting to do some meaningful work. We plan to evaluate his progress and will consider his participation in future shows."

But then something bizarre happened: Instead of Wallen's album sales dipping, they skyrocketed even more after he was a finalist, with many continuing to pity him. Wallen's second studio album, coincidentally titled *Dangerous: The Double Album,* spent over ten weeks at number one on Top Country Albums and ten weeks atop the all-genre Billboard 200. As if that wasn't enough, it would become the first country record to spend its first four weeks at number one since 2003. The album, which was released in early January of 2021, seemed to receive a boost from the controversy—which some claim was a result of his fans bucking against cancel culture.

Former Arkansas governor and Fox News contributor Mike Huckabee opined, "I suspect the real reason is not because they were showing support for using a racial slur but because they are fed up with the 'cancel culture' trying to destroy people's lives and careers because they made a dumb mistake for which they have publicly apologized."

Black country music star Mickey Guyton wrote about her support for Wallen on Twitter: "Watching anyone fall from grace is a terrible thing to see. People must all be given a chance to change. Morgan must feel the weight of his words but completely throwing someone away is detrimental to anyone's mental health."

His sister Ashlyne Wallen weighed in on Instagram with an argument that has become prevalent today: "[Cancel culture] leaves no room for forgiveness and growth, in turn, leaving no opportunity for individuals who have made mistakes to learn from them. If you make a mistake or do something stupid then apologize, correct your mistake, and learn through personal growth."

It's a fair conversation to debate how much grace we

should grant people who make mistakes, apologize, and express an intention to do better. But we should be honest about who gets offered this grace. When Southern cooking TV star Paula Dean admitted to saying the N-word in 2013, her career never recovered. When you try to equate the terms of what's cancelable, male privilege shapes the outcome. America was quick to cancel a white woman who used a racial slur but resisted terminating the career of an emerging male country star who did the same. It should be noted that perhaps Dean's cancellation was evident because it was during the Obama era, compared to Wallen's actions happening following Trump's era of political incorrectness. Even when you factor in critical and commercial success, the Chicks had multiple multi-platinum albums and Grammy awards long before their cancellation, and Dean was a household name with multiple TV shows and a product line—the fact that Wallen's career is thriving off his controversy speaks volumes.

Such glaring double standards aren't only issues within purely conservative spaces but in more progressive ones, too. At the time of their peak, both actor/singer Paul Robeson and singer/dancer Josephine Baker were international superstars. Some might take the success of these two Black performers as proof that they overcame whatever racism they faced in the world. However, they were also famous at a time when keeping your politics to yourself was expected for performers, particularly Black performers. Baker was disappointed by her options as a performer in the U.S. and moved to Paris in 1925, at the age of nineteen. She became an instant sensation for her daring performances, but eventually also became known for her politics. She was part of the Free France movement of World War II, and when she traveled to the U.S. to perform, she refused to play at segregated clubs and theaters. Robeson used his enormous celebrity to bring light to injustice. Like Baker, he refused to perform at segregated clubs and supported union efforts and urged President Truman to establish anti-lynching laws. Both Baker and Robeson faced consequences for their outspokenness. Baker's travel visa to the U.S. was revoked for ten years after she criticized the Stork Club for their racist policies and false rumors about Baker's affiliation with the Communist Party. Robeson's recordings and films were removed from distribution after he refused to sign an affidavit declaring that he was not a Communist.

While both Robeson and Baker had enormous status as celebrities, it was not enough to overpower racism. It's not only about what they spoke out about but who they were as people. Although both were progressive and, as artists, lived in progressive spaces, their lives intersected with a conservative ruling class. The people and organizations that tried to end their careers were conservatives who could not accept the outspokenness of Robeson or Baker. Digital strategist Leslie Mac says, "When we see folks like Paul Robeson—who was very open about his political perspectives and was most certainly canceled because of it, his career suffered, as did Josephine Baker's. Discussing cancel culture without the additional lens of power becomes futile."

The amount of power a person has or doesn't have when they enter the cancel zone will also play a part in the outcome. A culture that may expect women to walk a certain line may allow men more leniency. As I mentioned in the introduction, Chrisette Michele got canceled for performing at one of Trump's inaugural balls while Kanye West, who had more nefarious ties to Trump, was treated with more nuance, grace, and empathy. In fact, West, who had longtime connections with Trump while he was in office—Michele only did one performance and later made it clear she was never a Trumper—often received public sympathy, regardless of how he defied his audience's political views. Progressives and conservative thinkers latched on to the belief that West, a man who once called out George W. Bush in 2005 as someone who "doesn't care about Black people," was worthy of care and concern as he struggled with mental health issues.

After his then wife, Kim Kardashian, posted a plea for understanding and empathy surrounding West's struggle with bipolar disorder, West was met with far-flung support. Celebrities like Ellen Pompeo and Demi Lovato tweeted praise for both Kardashian and West and asked their fans to acknowledge how common mental illness is and not make entertainment out of West's outbursts.

On the difference between the reception that Michele and West received for affiliating with Trump, journalist William Ketchum III says, "I think three things drive that difference: how willing we are to live without what those people contribute to our lives, how those people make us feel about ourselves, and of course, the severity and timing of what they did. Kanye West dropped genre-shifting albums and established himself as a fashion icon before he went left, and people felt that he represented the peak of creativity and individuality; he's also spoken on behalf of Black and oppressed people early on in his career, so there was a long-term connection with his audience. . . . Chrisette Michele was a talented singer, but she wasn't a superstar; the only reason that Trump even reached out to her was because so many other celebrities had already refused," he adds. "So, her decision to sing at Trump's inauguration is the most definitive memory that many people have of her; she was easy to cancel because no one had any connection to her work that would've made it difficult to let her go."

"Kanye and Trump will never be permanently canceled because corporate media, both news and entertainment branches, benefit from them being untouchable and enduring even when they are mocked and ridiculed," says Dawn Ennis, a transgender journalist and professor. "The media is what drives that difference. Which cancellation benefits the corporations and their advertisers? Which one will consumers, including news consumers, love to hate, and which ones will they boycott?" Again, it comes back to status. Not only do Kanye and Trump have out-size status, but they also deliver status to others in the form of audiences and advertising dollars.

Activist and attorney Preston Mitchum puts an even finer point on it. "A few factors drive the differences be-tween those who are canceled and those who are not, in-cluding if a person has relative privilege. For example, wealth, access, resources, race, gender, sexual orientation and gender identity/expression, the person's proximity to whiteness, and how long we have known of a person, among others." In other words, the more expressions of power a person holds, the more likely they are to survive cancellation. It's not fair. The inequities of the world con-tinue to exist even when cancel culture is deployed. Can-cel culture is more art than science, and sometimes people who might deserve a second chance don't get it.

The consequences of these differences can be seen within the #MeToo movement. Powerful Black men who were alleged to have abused Black women weren't can-celed nearly as often as white men who have abused white women. In these scenarios, it's the status of the women involved that alter the outcome. With the notable excep-tions of disgraced entertainers Bill Cosby and R. Kelly, other Black men accused haven't faced the severe conse-quences of white celebrities like Harvey Weinstein, fired NBC news personality Matt Lauer, or ousted former CBS CEO Les Moonves. Hip-hop mogul Russell Simmons, who was the subject of an entire HBO documentary that aired in 2020 and detailed numerous sexual assault allegations against him, continues to be embraced by the music industry. Some Black women have accused him of blackballing them from that very industry. Rap superstar the Game continues to make new music and maintain a huge fan base on social media, despite a judge ordering him to pay a victim $7.13 million after being found guilty of sexual assault in 2016. Rapper Kodak Black never got canceled by his fans and the industry after avoiding prison time for allegedly raping a teenage girl in 2016 by pleading guilty to a lesser charge in April 2021. Boxing legend Floyd Mayweather continues to make millions, garner sponsorship deals, and win heavyweight titles despite being confronted with numerous domestic abuse charges over the years. These are just a few of the dozens of Black male athletes, rappers, and executives who have either been repeatedly accused or charged of abusing Black women and continue to be successful, nonetheless.

The outcries of white women have historically been given more attention and empathy than those of Black women. In 1991, when Black lawyer and academic Anita Hill accused Supreme Court nominee Clarence Thomas of sexual harassment, society canceled her at the time for what Thomas would describe as a "high-tech lynching" of his reputation as a Black man. This wasn't the experience of Dr. Christine Blasey Ford when she testified before the Senate Judiciary Committee in September 2018, accusing then Supreme Court nominee Brett Kavanaugh of sexually assaulting her when they were teenagers. Ford was praised in the media[10] and across the political aisle as being "credible" and would go on to grace the cover of *Time* magazine, and her testimony is claimed to have "changed America." Hill was judged harshly, her motivations were questioned, and she lived under media scrutiny long after Thomas was confirmed. In 1993, *American Spectator* writer David Brock mischaracterized Hill[11] in his flawed attempt to expose her "true motives" in his controversial book *The Real Anita Hill*. At the time, the book had received positive reviews and was excerpted by writers at *Newsweek, The Washington Post, The Wall Street Journal,* and *The New York Times,* with Jonathan Groner of *The Post*[12] describing it as "a serious work of investigative journalism." In June 2001, Brock would finally recant[13] the claims he made in his book, describing it as "character assassination" and apologizing to Hill. But the damage had been done. Hill had endured the pain of cancel culture for a decade from a society that never gave her the same level of consideration and empathy for her courage that they would later give Ford. Of course, time plays a role in the difference between Hill's and Ford's experiences. We understand harassment and assault so much better now than we did in the 1990s. However, the race of each woman cannot be discounted as a factor in their experience.

Therefore, it's critical to challenge the lack of intersectionality within cancel culture rather than presuming it is an evenly distributed action. The term *intersectionality* was conceptualized and coined in 1989 by Dr. Kimberlé Crenshaw, a Black scholar who also explored critical race theory. It delves into the interconnected nature of social categories such as race, class, and gender by recognizing how they apply to individuals or communities through the overlap of interdependent systems of marginalization. In other words, intersectionality digs into how various identities can create different experiences for people. Whereas all women across various racial and social communities demanded accountability during the #MeToo movement, Black and Brown women often received less public attention and support for their complaints in comparison to their white counterparts. The same can be said for the coverage and support white gay men received while they were protesting the Reagan administration during the HIV/AIDS crisis in the 1980s, compared to the attention Black queer and transgender people, who are disproportionately impacted by the epidemic, currently receive. Identity politics shape not only *why* people cancel but *how* cancel culture affects them. Racism, sexism, homophobia, ageism, and other forms of bias don't suddenly disappear the moment cancel culture takes place. In fact, it's often reinforced, given that it's being carried out by imperfect humans who can never leave their implicit—and in some instances, unconscious—biases at the door. By continuing to bring attention to inequalities, we can shape cancel culture into a gesture that helps more and more people.

In looking at America's cancellation of Janet Jackson in 2004 for her part in "Nipplegate" during the Super Bowl halftime show, it's hard to not consider the role race, gender, and age played into why she—and not Justin Timberlake, a young white man—was penalized. Jackson was an older Black woman who had embraced her sexuality for decades, an icon of entertainment, a member of pop royalty. Timberlake was a young white guy who had successfully crossed over from a boy band into a promising solo career. When the two set off the FCC alarm with their racy performance that culminated in Timberlake ripping away a piece of Jackson's nipple shield, exposing her bare breast, only one of them experienced the brunt of the shame and cancellation. Jackson was banned from the Grammys, and both MTV and VH1 banned her music. It's easy to call out how Timberlake benefited from white privilege and avoided being banned on television and radio, having major endorsement deals blocked, and being blacklisted by the industry in general. In fact, Timberlake was able to capitalize off the scandal by later shaping his image as "bringing sexy back," while Jackson was consistently slut-shamed and ridiculed by critics for going overboard.

People cancel things based on their perspective of the world—which is informed by what they know. For cancel culture to happen, there has to be a critical mass of those who are determined to act on something with a concerted, strategic effort. This approach, by default, can easily be manipulated based on privilege, access, and opportunity gaps. For example, those who were against Jim Crow segregation laws didn't have enough power to cancel them until technology and population shifts gave Black Americans the social mobility to fight back. When journalists began to cover the abuse of Black people on national television in the Deep South, that helped propel the movement for civil rights in ways that hadn't happened previously. The violence had always existed, the hate was always there. However, other factors had to be introduced into the dynamic to shift the narrative. Television and broadcast journalism coverage of the civil rights movement helped change the minds of some white Americans, including U.S. presidents and legislators, who had been on the fence about racial segregation before. The public exposure of bigotry forced many individuals to confront their own guilt and roles in the wrongdoing. Cancel culture, in this case, was propelled by the activists and the technological advancements that weren't there before. This new exposure to the realities of racism provided many Americans with a new perspective on their own country. As a result, a country that had once treated the separation of Black people from the rest of the country as the law of the land was now ready to cancel it.

Cancel culture is an evolution, not a permanent state

of being. The things we hold in high regard today can be canceled tomorrow. The people we once despised might be reimagined as being more insightful in the future. It took time, but the impression that people have of Janet Jackson now is not of someone who behaved inappropriately but rather as someone who was treated unfairly. In his prime, Dr. Martin Luther King Jr. and several Black leaders were listed as terrorists and spied on by the FBI's first director, J. Edgar Hoover.

"Hoover saw the civil rights movement from the 1950s onward and the anti-war movement from the 1960s onward as presenting the greatest threats to the stability of the American government since the Civil War," Pulitzer Prize–winning writer Tim Weiner said during an NPR interview[14] promoting his book *Legacy of Ashes* in 2012. "These people were enemies of the state, and in particular Martin Luther King [Jr.] was an enemy of the state. And Hoover aimed to watch over them. If they twitched in the wrong direction, the hammer would come down."

Today, most Americans invoke Dr. King's nonviolent rhetoric and activism as the gold standard for the public to follow. Once a national security risk and target of cancel culture, the renowned civil rights leader is now weaponized against current Black Lives Matter activists as being the "nonviolent" alternative—even though history once labeled him as a public enemy. These contradictions are a by-product of society's evolution. What was once praised as necessary censorship of women's sexuality is now viewed as excessive slut-shaming. Classic Disney films that included musical numbers featuring jiving crows and pipe-smoking Indigenous characters have gone from being labeled entertainment to being deemed racially offensive. A film celebrating the life and legacy of the leader of the Black Panthers can now win Oscars, a shift from when the organization was once considered a problematic, Black-extremist group in the twentieth century. What we canceled yesterday may be uncanceled today. Ask the Exonerated Five, formally known as the Central Park Five. What we praised years ago, we have now rejected. Ask America's once favorite TV dad, Bill Cosby.

History has reminded us that identity politics, shaped by power, position, and privilege, determines how things are canceled and why. It's an unfair system, given that imperfect people are determining things based on imperfect scales of value. It's the reason why society was quick to cancel a Black musical icon after her nipple slipped— but gave an Oscar to Woody Allen, a beloved white male filmmaker who was accused of sexually abusing his own adoptive daughter. This is why Republicans declined to hold Trumpers accountable for storming the Capitol Building on January 6, 2021, but made sure to demand that we "lock her up" when Hillary Clinton ran for president in 2016.

Cancel culture is biased, personal, and complicated. Just like our legal system, the arbitrators will not always get it right—but that's to be expected. The answer to the sometimes unequal way that cancel culture is leveraged is not to do away with it but to press on and keep highlighting inequities in the world. Cancel culture is not fair every time, but it does give so many people the chance to speak truth to power that it's ultimately worth it. No one will be surprised to hear that I do not approve of the ways—or the reasons why—conservatives cancel. And while I believe cancel culture is overall a force for good, that doesn't mean we should ignore the bigotry that seeps into it in some cases. The more that bigotry is highlighted—through all kinds of activism, including cancel culture—the more level a playing field we'll all be on. In its best form, cancel culture is a tool for democracy, and both cancel culture and democracy are complicated, sometimes messy, and essential to the American project.

CANCEL-CRY ME A RIVER

X X X X X X X X X X X X X

Current arguments against cancel culture are driven by
fear, misunderstanding, and sometimes an intentional
mischaracterization of how power works.

It's not possible to be involved in discussions around
cancel culture without being aware of its many detractors. Those detractors are not a monolith. In fact,
the criticisms of cancel culture are wide-ranging. Many
fear that cancel culture is a form of censorship, that it
will dilute complex issues, and that it robs us of joy and
humor. And perhaps the biggest knock on cancel culture
is that well-meaning people will be canceled by an online
mob and not given a chance to learn and grow.

I don't dismiss these concerns, at least, not all of them.
When good-faith arguments are made, it's reasonable
to engage in a debate about the pros and cons of cancel
culture. I've never claimed that cancel culture is without
drawbacks and limitations, as I explained in the "Not All
Cancellations Are the Same" chapter. I do, however, take
issue with bad-faith arguments around cancel culture,
which I see frequently. Let's go through the key arguments

(both good and bad faith) against cancel culture, and I'll explain why they don't hold up.

THE CENSORSHIP ARGUMENT

You might assume that a letter sent to House Judiciary chair Jerry Nadler[1] on March 1, 2020, that discussed the "dangerous trend" of "silencing and censoring certain political speech" was addressing the incendiary rhetoric that provoked the January 6 insurrection or the misinformation campaigns that were set off during the COVID-19 pandemic. But no. Republican congressman Jim Jordan of Ohio was requesting a hearing to "address the scourge of cancel culture"—something he felt was worth spending taxpayer money to investigate. "Cancel culture's long-term consequences to our democracy and our constitutional framework are serious and substantial," Jordan wrote in the letter, later adding that "we must fight this trend before it is too late."

This is the same Congressman Jordan who voted to overturn the 2020 presidential election results, even after Trump supporters stormed the nation's capital. Jordan even had the audacity to complain about the former president being banned from Twitter and Facebook for inciting the deadly riot. His claims about the dangers of cancel culture were used to deflect from his blind allegiance to Trump and the atrocities being conducted in his name. Undermining American democracy is no problem in Jordan's eyes, cancel culture is.

As I discussed in the "When Conservatives Cancel" chapter, conservatives have been so obsessed with the potential harm of cancel culture that they made the theme of the Conservative Political Action Conference (CPAC) "America Uncanceled." Republican leaders such as Jordan, Trump, and Ted Cruz deflected the criticism they had received for their part in the big lie as an attack on America itself. They believe—or want us to believe—they are patriots being censored. Conservatives, who had already begun to redefine cancel culture as a weapon used by progressives, were now framing it as an assault of American values overall: CPAC 2021 was their big-tent effort to collectively shift the narrative.

Senator Josh Hawley complained,[2] "Speaking of being canceled, the last six weeks, the radical left, their corporate allies, the liberal media, have tried to cancel me, censor me, expel me, shut me down, stop me from representing the people of Missouri, stop me from representing you." He went on to proclaim his defiance. "And guess what? I'm here today. I'm not going anywhere, and I'm not backing down. Not a chance, not a chance." Given that he'd led efforts to obstruct the Electoral College vote count for Biden, it makes sense that he'd rather people focus on just about anything else.

Not surprisingly, Trump also wanted to avoid the criticism he was facing. It was much better, in his estimation, to focus on the imagined dangers of cancel culture. "For the next four years, the brave Republicans in this room will be at the heart of the effort to oppose the radical Democrats, the fake news media, and their toxic cancel culture," Trump said during what many saw as a grand return-to-the-public-eye speech following the insurrection. "Something new to our ears, cancel culture. And I want you to know that I'm going to continue to fight right by your side. We will do what we've done right from the beginning, which is to win."

In fact, the conference canceled the appearance of Black self-proclaimed artist and philosopher Young Pharaoh, who was supposed to be part of a panel called "Please Check the Number and Dial Again: Doubt, Dysfunction, and the Price of Missed Opportunities" after complaints that he was anti-Semitic. "Young Pharaoh uses his platform to spread horrific antisemitic lies," the American Jewish Committee, a global Jewish advocacy organization, wrote in a statement at the time. "He has no place on the [CPAC] stage. CPAC leadership must denounce his antisemitic conspiracy theories and act to ensure that Jew-hatred has no place at the conference."

CPAC quickly responded[3] by tweeting, "We have just learned that someone we invited to CPAC has expressed reprehensible views that have no home with our conference or our organization. The individual will not be participating at our conference."

The irony of a conference whose theme was to call

out cancel culture—while canceling someone's appearance at the same time—is hilarious. Never mind the fact that many of the speakers at the event were calling on attendees to not support, listen to, or engage with certain politicians who were not willing to support the big lie. Never mind the fact that Trump used the event to target[4] fellow conservatives, listing, "Mitt Romney, little Ben Sasse, Richard Burr, Bill Cassidy, Susan Collins, Lisa Murkowski, Pat Toomey—and in the House, Tom Rice, South Carolina, Adam Kinzinger, Dan Newhouse, Anthony Gonzalez, that's another beauty, Fred Upton, Jaime Herrera Beutler, Peter Meijer, John Katko, David Valadao, and of course, the warmonger, a person that loves seeing our troops fighting, Liz Cheney." It was clear that while conservatives at CPAC wanted "American Uncanceled," they still wanted to reserve the right to cancel when it suited them.

Critics outside of politics also equate cancel culture with censorship and used the words interchangeably. "Unfortunately, too many on the left, wielding the cudgel of 'cancel culture,' have decided that certain forms of censorship and speech and idea suppression are positive things that will advance social justice," Dan Kovalik, a human rights lawyer and free speech advocate, argues in his 2021 book[5] *Cancel This Book: The Progressive Case Against Cancel Culture*. "I fear that those who take this view are in for a rude awakening."

For the record, none of the politicians listed here were

facing blowback for speaking their truth. On the contrary, they were being criticized for lying about the election and encouraging protestors to force a change in the results. How can they claim censorship when they've been able to tell these lies over and over? And it was not the "radical Left" that was calling them out but the mainstream media and many apolitical Americans. It doesn't make sense for Dan Kovalik to be so concerned with speaking his mind if he was able to publish an entire book about his cancel culture philosophy. This link between cancel culture and censorship has been repeated so often that many Americans accept them as one and the same, but they are not. In fact, cancel culture allows for *more* people to speak their truth, not fewer.

THE DILUTION ARGUMENT

Closely related to the censorship argument is the dilution argument. In these cases, critics fear that complex intellectual discussion will be done away with in favor of rigid thinking due to cancel culture. This harkens back to the era of political correctness of the late 1980s and 1990s.

"A Letter on Justice and Open Debate" published by *Harper's Magazine* is a high-profile example of this argument. Signed by such cultural heavyweights as Gloria Steinem, Noam Chomsky, Malcom Gladwell, Cornel

West, David Brooks, and J. K. Rowling, the letter spelled out the concern that "the free exchange of information of ideas, the lifeblood of a liberal society, is daily becoming more constricted," continuing that: "an intolerance of opposing views, a vogue for public shaming and ostracism and the tendency to dissolve complex policy issues in a blinding moral certainty." The group insisted on the importance of writers being allowed to experiment, take risks, and even make mistakes.

When the negative reactions to the letter started, some of the signatories expressed regret. Transgender author Jennifer Finney Boylan was moved to speak out[6] about the letter after her fans questioned her signing with famed author-turned-alleged-transphobe J. K. Rowling. "I did not know who else had signed that letter. I thought I was endorsing a well-meaning, if vague, message against internet shaming. I did know Chomsky, Steinem, and Atwood were in, and I thought, good company. The consequences are mine to bear. I am so sorry."

Some spoke out about having been asked to sign the letter and deciding to stay out of it. "I declined to sign the Harper's letter because Trumpism, racism, xenophobia, and sexism have had such free rein and baleful influence in recent years that we should honor and respect the expressions of anger and heartache finally being heard," tweeted author, professor, and former U.S. secretary of labor Robert Reich when backlash against the letter took off. It's a remarkable thing to hear cancel culture being described so eloquently by someone like Reich, a privileged, older, straight white man.

It's clear to me that many of these boomer-and-older signatories have, at best, an unsteady grasp on what cancel culture is and, at worst, a blind spot for their own power and prestige. Here they are, a group of mostly ultra-successful, ultra-influential people publishing a letter outlining their intellectual concerns in one of the most highly regarded magazines in the world—and *they're* worried about cancel culture?

It's not only the senior members of the cultural elite who fear cancel culture's powers of dilution. Then college journalist Emma Camp wrote a self-pitying op-ed[7] for *The New York Times* on March 7, 2022, called "I Came to College Eager to Debate. I Found Self-Censorship Instead." Camp describes feeling uncomfortable in class when expressing opinions that may be unpopular. She's fearful of being ostracized but doesn't seem to have experienced it. And in the piece's most convoluted thinking, she asks for the unlimited right to make her thoughts known but wants protection against a reaction to those thoughts. She insists that she doesn't mind being disagreed with but contradicts herself by describing how silenced she felt by her classmate's displeasure with her opinions. She complains about being on the business end of a Twitter pile-on when fellow University of Virginia students objected to her op-ed about free speech. To be clear, no one stopped

Camp from publishing anything. They were utilizing their own free speech to argue with Camp—which, on the face of it, is what she's in favor of. In the end, Camp's point seems to be that she should be able to say what she wants and everyone else should be nicer to her.

THE MOB MENTALITY ARGUMENT

The fear of an angry online mob is a sentiment that's often associated with cancel culture. And while the internet can be a highly uncivilized place, it's not the fault of cancel culture, despite what critics might claim.

"Liberals need a Stand Your Ground law . . . for cancel culture," liberal media personality Bill Maher said[8] during a February 2021 episode of his hit television show *Real Time with Bill Maher.* "So that when the woke mob comes after you for some ridiculous offense, you'll stand your ground, stop apologizing. Because I can't keep up with who's on the shitlist." Maher, who has never been shy of sparking controversy, went as far as to claim that conservatives are "trying to appropriate" what cancel culture means as being something that "happens to them when they get a just comeuppance for actual crimes." I would agree with Maher's characterization of how conservatives frame cancel culture, except he believes the real problem is going to be faced by everyone. He described the actions from the Right as "unfortunate" because "cancel culture is real, it's insane, it's growing exponentially, coming to a neighborhood near you." On this point, Maher is just wrong. Cancel culture is not coming to a neighborhood near you.

On his show, Maher told viewers to "think about everything you've ever texted, emailed, searched for, tweeted, blogged, or said in passing. Or now even just witnessed. 'Someone had a Confederate flag in their dorm room in 1990 and you didn't do anything?' 'You laughed at a Woody Allen movie?'

"Everybody hates it, but nobody stands up to it," Maher further complained to the audience. "Because it's always the safe thing to swallow what you really think and just join the mob. Mature people understand humans are continually evolving as opposed to Wokeville, where they're always shocked, we didn't emerge enlightened from the primordial ooze," he protested. "Memo to social justice warriors: When what you're doing sounds like an *Onion* headline, stop."

It makes sense that those with more power and influence would describe the experience of being called out as a "mob." For high-profile people, thousands of their fans, followers, and audiences may respond negatively to something problematic they've done. This doesn't happen to average people, who are rarely "canceled" in the same vein. Sure, there are outlier situations in which everyday people can go viral for problematic behavior, leading to them losing a job or being publicly criticized by large groups of people, but these are highly unlikely in the grand scheme of things. Cancel culture usually comes for the most powerful individuals and institutions.

Those who disapprove of a high-profile person's problematic behavior don't just transform into an angry, woke Twitter mob. They are individuals who have likely invested in the public figure's overall success, fame, and power. The most powerful want us to think that fans who aren't blindly loyal to them become enemies, engaging in a mob mentality. The "if you're not with us, you're against us" ethos is what drives fearmongering around cancel culture. This rhetoric is a form of bullying, meant to intimidate those from speaking out about things they believe. Black Lives Matter activists are now being called the *woke police*, LGBTQIA people who speak out against homophobia and transphobia are framed as "intolerant" of those who don't agree with them, feminists are labeled "man-eaters," "man-bashers," and "man-haters," simply for calling for the end of sexism, and any coalition of people who criticize, boycott, or protest are depicted an unprincipled and unruly "mob" who lack morals, fairness, and tact. These labels were in the public consciousness before "Twitter mobs" and "woke police" were a trend—they were the ways that the powerful tried to stifle the free speech of those who were fighting for their right to exist.

Sadly, the most powerful will try to make themselves relatable, making it seem like the average person is as vulnerable to cancel culture as they are. Plus, it's been effective. Many people have real concerns that they'll be shamed or even fired for missteps or mistakes in their pasts. In an age where your digital history is permanent, it's wise to be thoughtful about what you put out there. Not just from a covering-your-ass perspective but from the point of view of accuracy, civility, and harm reduction. It's not phony to consider how your words might affect others. Isn't how we live, communicate, and behave a reflection of our character and our morals? In more plain language: Don't be a jerk.

The truth is: The average person is not being canceled. It's people or organizations with power and status, which is why the rich and famous are often the ones turning accountability into something despicable—they're the ones with something to lose. Creating an imagined enemy is a classic way of deflecting responsibility. Rather than debate the details of the case, conservatives described efforts to impeach Trump as being a "witch hunt." Ronald Reagan dismissed growing concern about Americans requiring government assistance by talking about "welfare queens," suggesting there were people living it up on their welfare checks. In each of these scenarios, the most powerful had to reset the terms of accountability. Rather than focus on their problematic actions, they had to find a new group to target—the people. But rather than directly attack the public, such influential people created ambiguous terms and phrases that would make everyday individuals rally behind them.

The other enduring complaint about the "woke mob" is the false framing of helplessness that people will find themselves in. "Cancel culture promotes a mob mentality that is often toxic because it gives people online a power they have never experienced before," wrote columnist Tania Ortiz[9] in a September 2020 op-ed for *The Cougar Chronicle*. "The power they possess is informal since social media users can unfollow and choose to ignore the person whom they are canceling."

It's true that social media allows people to jump on a bandwagon—and sometimes even harass—and create what cancel culture haters call the "Twitter mob" or the "woke mob." However, Ortiz reveals herself how lacking in potency this really is. Being attacked by someone or some group on Twitter? Block them. *Problem solved.*

THE INNOCENCE ARGUMENT

The argument that goes hand in hand with the fear of the mob is the fear that innocent people will be caught up in the cancel culture frenzy and be irreparably harmed.

"I constantly encounter students who are so fearful of being subjected to the Twitter mob that they are engaging in self-censorship," said former ACLU president Nadine

Strossen during a January 2021 nonpartisan virtual panel[10] called "The Case Against Cancel Culture" that was hosted by the Pacific Legal Foundation. I don't doubt that this is true. The mainstream media, celebrities, and politicians of all stripes have so loudly and consistently crowed about the dangers of cancel culture that it makes sense that people fear it.

Trump added fuel to the fire at the 2020 Republican National Convention: "The goal of cancel culture is to make decent Americans live in fear of being fired, expelled, shamed, humiliated and driven from society as we know it." One delegate resolution at the event defined cancel culture as being responsible for "erasing history, encouraging lawlessness, muting citizens, and violating free exchange of ideas, thoughts, and speech."

As I discussed in the "Cancel Culture Been Here" chapter, what goes largely unacknowledged is the way that cancel culture has been with humanity from the beginning. If anything has been erased from history, it is the existence of cancel culture. And, as I've stated previously, everyday "decent Americans" don't have anything to fear in cancel culture—they do not have the status that's required to be canceled.

Examples of everyday people being canceled are often not really cancellations at all. The first, and possibly most famous, example of this was Justine Sacco.[11] A PR exec at the high-profile corporate governance consulting firm IAC, Sacco was on her way to South Africa to visit family when she tweeted, "Going to Africa. Hope I don't get AIDS. Just kidding. I'm white!" By the time she landed, her tweet and the outrage over it had gone viral, and Sacco was fired, an international pariah. Yes, it's an extreme consequence, but when Justine Sacco embarrassed a company whose job it is to advise on corporate behavior, what choice did they have? Not only did Sacco's behavior make her look bad, but her employer was also being called out on social media, too. Stating that Sacco's tweet went against their views and values, IAC announced they had parted ways. This was a human resources situation, not a cancel culture situation.

More recently, Amy Cooper, known as the "Central Park Karen," lost her job at Franklin Templeton insurance firm after a video went viral of her calling 911 on Black bird-watcher Christian Cooper (no relation, obviously) in 2021. She and her off-leash dog were in a part of Central Park called the Ramble, which is popular with bird-watchers. Dogs must be kept on leash in this area. When Christian Cooper asked her to leash her dog, Amy Cooper called 911 and cried that she was being threatened by an "African American" man. Christian Cooper used his phone[12] to take a video of the altercation, knowing full well the danger she was putting him in. Explaining why he chose to film, he told NBC News, "I'm not going to participate in my own dehumanization. We live in an age of Ahmaud Arbery, where Black men are gunned down because of assumptions people make about Black men, Black people, and I'm just not going to participate in that." Ahmaud Arbery, of course, is the Black man who was shot while jogging, unarmed. Amy Cooper's employer made a statement about her dismissal, reading, "We do not tolerate racism of any kind at Franklin Templeton."

In both scenarios, and many others like them, it's possible for the central figures to cry cancel culture, but it would not be correct. Many, if not most, workplaces have codes of conduct, and yes, they do apply to time spent outside of work. Or, as Kate Bischoff,[13] an employment lawyer and HR consultant with k8bisch LLC, told *The Wall Street Journal* in July 2020, "Don't be dumb, because if you're dumb, it's going to reflect negatively on us." Employers have wide latitude to terminate people for their words and actions. For the same article, Stacy Hawkins, a law professor at Rutgers University, said, "A private employer doesn't have to protect your free-speech rights, only the government has to do that." Rather than being the victim of cancel culture, both Justine Sacco and Amy Cooper received the predictable consequences of their own actions.

THE "NO GRACE" ARGUMENT

It has been argued that cancel culture is too harsh; that if people make mistakes, they should be given an opportunity to learn and grow and be gently educated. Of course, this generously assumes that people being canceled are making mistakes rather than simply saying or doing what they believe is right. When you are well known, of course, a lot of people are going to see your "mistakes."

"Being a public figure today seems to require a certain level of direct access to you by the public," says notable digital strategist and organizer Leslie Mac. "If we are comparing to days gone by where celebrities and public figures' personal lives and opinions were largely made up by PR machines, holding a fake persona accountable was impossible." For some, this is a new world. If you became famous forty years ago, this new need for transparency is likely shocking. For those who are more recently known, they've entered their position understanding what would be required of them—or they should.

Chrissy Teigen, media personality and wife of progressive singer John Legend, was once considered the "Queen of Twitter" for her bold critiques on conservatives, pop culture, and just about anything she couldn't stand. She seemed like the least likely person ever to find herself getting canceled. In fact, her following rallied to her defense after Alison Roman, a popular white food writer, made some offensive remarks about Teigen's rise in the culinary world, along with other anti-Asian "jokes" in 2020. Teigen's own brash attacks against Trump on social media, speaking out against racism, sexism, and other forms of hate, made her appear as one of the most relatable and socially conscious celebrities in pop culture. Roman took a pounding on social media and lost work because of her ugly remarks.

But the public adulation all came crashing down for Teigen in May 2021 after nonbinary model Courtney Stodden revealed[14] hurtful and cruel tweets and direct messages they received from Teigen as a teenager. "She wouldn't just publicly tweet about wanting me to take 'a dirt nap' but would privately DM me and tell me to kill myself," Stodden told the Daily Beast in an interview. "Things like, 'I can't wait for you to die.'" It's hard to imagine why Teigen thought it was in any way appropriate to send a DM to anyone telling them to have a "dirt nap" (die, in other words) and that she had to be called out about it publicly before she apologized.

The backlash for Teigen was huge, with many of her fans on social media pulling their support from her, along with major brands and endorsers. For example, Macy's removed Teigen's cookware line from its website, and the celebrity even dropped out of a voice role for the Netflix teen series *Never Have I Ever*. Although Teigen offered a public apology and took a break from social media, cancel culture finally caught up to her. She experienced the very level of consequence she has called for others to pay in the past.

Disappointingly, just like many who whine about cancel culture and play the blame game, Teigen did the same thing.[15] Cancel culture is the weakness of the most powerful and influential, regardless of their political ideology. "Cancel club is a fascinating thing and I have learned a wholllle lot. Only a few understand it and it's impossible to know til you're in it," Teigen dramatically wrote on her Instagram page in July 2021, with a nonchalant photo of her legs in ripped jeans. "And it's hard to talk about it in that sense because obviously you sound whiny when you've clearly done something wrong. It just sucks. There is no winning. But there never is here anyhow," she protested.

It was hard to take Teigen seriously. She had been posting photos from a family trip to Italy, saying that going outside during her cancellation "sucks and doesn't feel right," but "being at home alone with my mind makes my depressed head race. I feel lost and need to find my place again, I need to snap out of this. I desperately wanna communicate with you guys instead of pretending everything is okay. I'm not used to any other way!!" she begged.

Imagine being a multimillionaire who gets to travel around the world with your EGOT-winning husband and whining to your over thirty million Instagram followers about how you're in "cancel club." Imagine thinking that your inability to be still and reflect on the problematic things you've done to others is a real-life crisis your fans really care to hear about from you. Imagine doing that while spending a luxurious summer in Italy. *Must be pretty damn nice.*

So often when people—particularly rich and famous

people—complain about cancel culture, it turns out they're just fine. Despite the drama she brought on herself, Teigen remains rich, famous, and mostly popular.

On the education front, blogger Vidal D'costa wrote[16] for *The Times of India,* "While cancel culture may seem like the modern weapon of choice because we find it easier to boycott and sweep ignorant people under the carpet, it is better to opt for education as it is a more appropriate, sensible, even classy method and is less harmful to all involved."

D'costa is not entirely wrong. Education can be a better route than cancellation. That's why most people try it first. Cancel culture happens when all else fails, and it's misleading to suggest that a person who makes sexist or racist remarks, for example, couldn't possibly have known better.

Whose job is it to educate those in power to do better? It's not like the material that would help people learn and do better isn't out there. There are resources in the form of books, documentaries, articles, YouTube videos, Twitter accounts, and so on. However, what often occurs is that the people who have been offended or antagonized are called upon to do the job. "Here's the hard truth: The vast majority of people who are called on do not want to be held accountable," says activist/attorney Preston Mitchum. "Accountability is not a quick and easy process: It takes time, attention, resources, and self-reflection. While I understand the position that no one should be thrown away, I also believe that not everyone is responsible for transforming others' harmful behaviors."

THE "NO FUN" ARGUMENT

Critics of cancel culture want you to think that it's the end of funny. Because, I guess, you can't be funny without being able to offend somebody. As always, keep an eye on who is making this argument.

"Especially now, the left, they are shrill. They are angry," Senator Ted Cruz griped[17] during his CPAC speech, obnoxiously titled "Bill of Rights, Liberty, and Cancel Culture." Cruz didn't want to talk about anything substantial—he just wanted to make it clear that cancel culture is a drag. He went on, "How many leftists does it take to screw in a light bulb? 'That's not funny!' God bless, who would want to be around these people? Jerry Seinfeld doesn't tell comedy anymore because any joke that's funny is canceled. *SNL* is unwatchable. The late-night comedy, they stand up and say, 'We hate Donald Trump,' Yeah, no kidding. We didn't get that the last 9,000 times you told that."

Cruz complaining that life's no fun anymore because of cancel culture is really him telling on himself. What exactly would he like to say that he can't? Do you need to be able to offend people to be funny?

Some creators now claim that they feel limited by the

growing dissent of their fans and marginalized communities. Who would have ever thought that *not* making racist jokes about Asians and homophobic remarks about queer people would stifle creative expression? To hear some comedians and celebrities talk about it, cancel culture means the death of coolness and joy as we know it.

"Cancel culture is stopping comedians taking risks, playing around and letting themselves fall," wrote stand-up comedian Shappi Khorsandi in a 2021 op-ed[18] titled "Cancel Culture Is Ruining Comedy—It's Time to Stand-Up to It" for *The Independent*. "Twitter, that screaming pit of merciless voices, is making comedy monochrome."

"You're all woke and no joke," griped veteran comedian Adam Carolla[19] about millennials and Gen Zers during a Comedy Central roast of Alec Baldwin in 2019. "So, if you were offended by anything said tonight, please give a reach around to your emotional support dog and shut the fuck up! This is our safe space, bitches." Carolla, a staunch conservative, would later go on to troll the youth once more in the 2019 film *No Safe Spaces*, in which he and nationally syndicated radio host Dennis Prager visit college campuses and attempt to frame cancel culture as the root cause of decades of censorship that has ruined American expression.

Baldwin himself clearly agrees. "Cancel culture is like a forest fire in constant need of fuel," tweeted the Emmy-

winning actor, who has previously defended the likes of
New York governor Andrew Cuomo and director Woody
Allen. "Functioning objectively. No prejudice. No code.
Just destroy. The deserving and the undeserving alike."

It harkens back to the 1980s and 1990s when people would lament political correctness and how nobody
could take a joke anymore. And yet comedy continued
after political correctness was the boogeyman of the day.
And comedy continues today. On Netflix alone, you can
find over two hundred comedy specials right now.

It makes sense that what is funny to people depends
on many different factors and shifts over time. The your-
money-or-your-wife jokes of the 1950s would be sexist
now. They would also just not be that funny anymore.
White audiences used to laugh at the stereotypical portrayals of Black men on *The Amos 'n' Andy Show*—
portrayals that would be horrifying to a contemporary
sensibility. And not all comics use the fear of cancel culture as an excuse. "It's weird when you're a comedian, because when you're a comedian, when the audience doesn't
laugh, we get the message. You don't really have to cancel
us because we get the message. They're not laughing," said
legendary entertainer Chris Rock while being a guest on
an episode of *The Breakfast Club* in 2021. "Our feelings
hurt. When we do something and people aren't laughing,
we get it. I don't understand why people feel the need to
go beyond that, you know what I mean?" the *Saturday*

Night Live star continued. "Honestly, to me, it's a disrespect. It's people disrespecting the audience like, 'Oh, you think you know more than the audience?'"

THE POWER ARGUMENT

This one is mine. I've said it before, and I'll say it again: Cancel culture has always been about power. Those who seek to take it, and those who are striving to redistribute it. Activism, boycotts, calls to exile, and protests have always been rooted in shifting—or maintaining—the power dynamics of a society. Those who complain about cancel culture are often fearful of its impact on their power and livelihoods. Money, fame, capital, and position are all threatened by cancel culture. The most influential people of the world understand what's at the root of cancel culture, but would rather misrepresent it in the public, hoping to make everyone despise it. These powerful people believe they can make the rest of us buy their false framing of cancel culture. And if everyday people can be made to fear being canceled in their own lives, they're likely to take a dim view of it. Why would the most powerful embolden others to use a tactic that could potentially hurt them? Cancel culture is a public figure's kryptonite, and for good reason.

Joe Rogan, media provocateur,[20] is a master of framing cancel culture as a danger to all. On his popular podcast, he said in May 2021, "You can never be woke enough, that's the problem. It keeps going, it keeps going further and further and further down the line, and if you get to the point where you capitulate, where you agree to all these demands, it'll eventually get to a point where straight white men aren't allowed to talk because it's your privilege to express yourself when other people of color have been silenced throughout history. It'll be, 'You're not allowed to go outside because so many people were imprisoned for so many years.' I'm not joking, it really will get there. It's that crazy."

Sure, Joe—because nothing spells cancel culture more than straight white men fearing that they are now an endangered species in a world that continues to benefit them more than any other demographic on earth. Giving underprivileged people increased rights won't automatically take away others' privilege. This is not a zero-sum game.

Rogan, who, at the time I'm writing this, is currently being paid $200 million by Spotify to regularly voice his wild opinions and conspiracies, went on to suggest how much cancel culture has been used as a way for others to build their own clout. In other words, if you are engaging in cancel culture, according to Rogan, you're just doing it for attention. "You know, we've just got to be nice to each other, man," Rogan suggested. "There's a lot of people that are taking advantage of the weirdness in our culture, and then that becomes their thing. Their thing is calling people out for their privilege, calling people out for their position."

If by "thing," Rogan means activism, then yes, that's a thing. And sure, some people might be hoping to gain attention by speaking out. That doesn't mean they're not genuine. Is Rogan—or any high-profile person—really in a position to criticize people wanting their opinions heard?

As a straight white man, Rogan clearly doesn't want to be told about his white male privilege and asked to stop leveraging it in ways that further marginalize people of color, women, and LGBTQIA individuals. Nor does he care for the criticisms he faced over the potential harm he caused with his anti-vax stance. Instead, powerful people like Rogan want to reduce such disputes to respectability politics around "niceness"—which is a tactic often used by those trying to gaslight victims. It's easy to deflect the conversation by focusing on the tone and tenor of those questioning your privilege rather than looking at actual racial and social inequity. Unfortunately for Rogan, his own cry-me-a-river moment arrived in early 2022, when multiple videos were found showing Rogan using the N-word.

Is that how we should be nice to each other, Joe?

Social media has complicated things. We have a love-hate relationship with digital platforms—we're addicted to them, and we blame them for every ill. Cancel culture has now been thrown into the pot of potential online harms and is often served to the public hot and steamy. Yes, social media has certainly fueled cyberbullying, online trolling, and harassment. And cancel culture is none of those things. But given that the most powerful want to avoid criticism—it's convenient for them to equate *any* form of online criticism (which inappropriately conflates bullying, trolling, and harassment as forms of accountability) with cancel culture. Social media has also opened the door to new levels of democracy. More than ever, people can engage in public discourse, and a new kind of governance has developed that we can all participate in.

Cancel culture has become the catchall buzzword because people have gotten too lazy to make proper distinctions, to draw lines, and to acknowledge legitimate pushback from the public. Too many critics of cancel culture spend more time worrying about the offender being canceled than asking why such a cancellation was made in the first place. The truth is that most people who get canceled did something to deserve it. They were in the wrong and they got caught. And given the amount of status you need to have to truly get canceled, I just can't feel that sorry about it.

So, you know, cry me a river.

CANCEL CULTURE IS DEMOCRACY UNCHAINED

Cancel culture is more than just a tool for accountability. It is a
deliberate form of free speech that works to liberate us all.

W here the waterline is gonna land on freedom of speech, what we allow and what
we don't, where this cancel culture goes, is
a very interesting place that we're engaged in as a society and are trying to figure out. We haven't found the
right spot," Oscar-winning actor Matthew McConaughey
told cohosts[1] Susanna Reid and Piers Morgan on *Good
Morning Britain* in December 2020. "I would argue we
don't have true confrontation right now, confrontation
that gives some validation and legitimizes the opposing
point of view. We don't give a legitimacy or validation to
an opposing point of view, we make it persona non grata,
and that's unconstitutional."

McConaughey, who prides himself on being "aggressively centric" on the political spectrum, has made
it a point to actively condemn cancel culture as being
antagonistic to democracy. In his view, progressives are
"arrogant," and he blames cancel culture and "illiberals"

(the name McConaughey gives to what he considers the extreme Left) for the current political divide in America. "And what I don't think that some liberals see is that they're often being cannibalized by the illiberals." McConaughey went on to describe how "the two extremes illegitimize those two sides. Or they exaggerate that side's stance into an irrational state that makes no sense and that's not fair when either side does that."

It would have been easier for McConaughey to just admit that he drank the conservative Kool-Aid. For a man like McConaughey—straight, white, American, and rich—to suggest that cancel culture is undemocratic reveals his privilege in believing that our current mechanisms of free speech are equal across the board. News flash: Cancel culture as we currently know it wouldn't exist if it were.

When people, often those who are white and privileged, challenge the democratic nature of cancel culture, they misinterpret exactly how free speech works. The Constitution is praised for having a Bill of Rights that grants citizens the First Amendment right of free speech. We can peacefully protest, write, debate, assemble, and say whatever we want without the government actively suppressing our right to do so, but what people fail to realize is that First Amendment rights protect citizens from the government's intervention, not the public's perception. In other words, the First Amendment holds the government accountable in how a person can utilize free speech, *not how the rest of society perceives that speech.*

For example, the First Amendment allows for people to make racial slurs and use other forms of hate speech without arrest—but it doesn't stop others from criticizing those who make those slurs. America allows for people to express themselves freely, to the point that many individuals assume they are protected from any consequences. The most powerful and privileged among us are struggling to understand the limitations of their First Amendment rights in an era where cancel culture is prominent.

"We have reinterpreted the First Amendment as an instrument for us to speak and to be heard and to mobilize in different ways, and certainly it has that application, but that was not its initial intent," says media scholar and advocate Meredith D. Clark, Ph.D. "And I think that that's very important to keep in mind, because people will raise First Amendment criticisms and objections as though they should somehow be shielded from criticism—or as though the things that they say are covered by the First Amendment because the First Amendment exists—and the very simple analysis of this belief is that's simply not how that works.

"The First Amendment and its interpretation, again, in legal precedent, has created space for people to be able to speak in ways that others might find offensive, that in some cases may be harmful," she adds. "These interpretations are late adaptations of how we've come to understand and apply the First Amendment at its core."

Before Black people were seen as full American citizens, LGBTQIA individuals weren't viewed as mentally ill, and women were allowed to own a credit card, powerful straight white men were allowed to be bigots without any consequences. Their First Amendment right to speak hatred without federal consequence was complemented by their ability to suppress marginalized communities via laws such as Jim Crow. America was cosigning white supremacy, sexism, and homophobia with policies that suppressed everyone that wasn't a straight white man. Back in the day, it wouldn't have been appalling for a white man to go to work in the morning and then put on a Ku Klux Klan hood at night and harass Black people. First Amendment rights were not extended to the rest of society until the Civil Rights Act of 1964, when the U.S. government finally decided that people of various backgrounds should also not be discriminated against based on race, religion, gender, and creed. It should be noted that LGBTQIA people are still waiting for the Equality Act to pass to be granted such sweeping protections as well.

The Civil Rights Act of 1964 was a key moment in contemporary cancel culture. It was in this moment that predominately white power structures couldn't overtly discriminate against the rest of society via free speech without potential consequence. Prior to the civil rights movement, Black people's concerns weren't given much public debate or consideration—a white man's word was simply the law. In many ways, that remains true, given how hard it is to overturn decades of entrenched white supremacy—but the ability to see a power struggle today is the result of cancel culture.

Cancel culture was the form of free speech the powerless couldn't fully utilize until after their civil rights were protected by law. The value of free speech under Jim Crow laws was compromised because the system had designed it that way. Martin Luther King Jr. could criticize segregation, but also face further discrimination and arrest for doing so. There was no accountability back then for anyone in power who had decided that marginalized people would have to wait for change, and for many decades, people in America had to wait for some resistance to finally kick in and force change.

That struggle continues, but no longer as passively. Cancel culture has leveled the playing field for those who can't always rely on the government to protect them. Right now, bigots are protected under the First Amendment, allowing them to fuel disgusting rhetoric without state-sanctioned consequence. The America that tolerated white supremacy in their policies and laws is the same country that wants to remind us how such forms of hate are still legal via free speech. Cancel culture is the poison to those in power that have benefited from unchecked free speech.

When conservatives on Fox News declare that it's a "free country" and that cancel culture is "un-American," they forget the double-edged sword that the First Amendment provided marginalized people once they got a slice of the free speech pie. Free speech works two ways: It allows for discourse to take place but grants all voices can be heard. In other words, straight white men and other people with power aren't used to getting pushback for the ways they conduct themselves—and cancel culture has reset the ways society can react.

When British media personality Piers Morgan publicly attacked[2] Meghan Markle, the Duchess of Sussex, on a March 2021 episode of *Good Morning Britain,* he didn't expect the immediate backlash or that he'd soon be exiting the show. Morgan slammed Markle for seeming to criticize the royal family and complaining about the bigotry she faced within the family and from the British press. Many viewed Morgan's comments as insensitive to Markle's mental health and racially insensitive, given the racist coverage she'd faced from the British tabloids as a Black woman. The station received over fifty-seven thousand complaints regarding Morgan's comments from disappointed viewers, including one from Markle herself. Public pressure is speculated to have played a role in Morgan abruptly leaving *Good Morning Britain* after nearly six years on the air.

In a previous era, Morgan would have been able to keep his job and those who complained about his comments wouldn't have been heard. The broadcaster would have been able to manage the messaging around Morgan's comments, as well as the public's reaction to them. But cancel culture is fueled by social media, so people who have traditionally been ignored can now insist on accountability. In many ways, cancel culture is reinforcing what our world would look like if everyone got a chance to weigh in on the issues and individuals that have power. Prior to social media and civil rights advancements, men like Morgan would have gone unchallenged. Today, he is put in a position to have to reckon with his behavior—even if he still gets to remain rich with some level of influence.

As I've said earlier in the book, cancel culture as we consider it today feels new because of the digital platforms we have at our disposal to speak truth to power. Previous generations were canceling—but the road to accountability was paved with many barriers, both technologically and socially. It was hard to fully cancel something when you weren't granted the same civil rights as your opponent—even more so when you could face even more persecution and exile for doing it. Once the internet began to take off in the 1990s, society began to see a shift in how the public could consider canceling with less gatekeeping. In 1997, the Supreme Court acknowledged[3] this major shift when it dealt with its first internet-related First Amendment case. The court wrote at the time that "any person with a phone line can become a town crier with a voice that resonates farther than it could from any soapbox."

Cancel culture has empowered everyday people with the opportunity to take a rejected letter to the editor and post it online, to digitally assemble a counterprotest when a physical permit isn't permissible, and to potentially overturn a decision after corporate bigwigs thought they had the final say. Today, the class of people who have ruled over us for centuries now have to confront a new normal. The powerful must accept that their word is no longer the final word. That final word now belongs to the masses. Cancel culture has kept the conversation going when it used to be cut short by those who once called and controlled the shots. A redistribution of power via social media has democratized the entire way in which we seek and define accountability—something that is more democratic than anything we have experienced before.

Cancel culture elevates democracy because it allows more people access to free speech, accountability, and public discourse. American political philosophy suggests, even if it has never fully realized it, that a society that gives every individual the opportunity to make their voices heard is ideal. We hear this rhetoric every time we cast a vote at the ballot box and are reminded of our freedoms during Independence Day. We should also remember the hypocrisy of marginalized people finally being granted rights they should have had all along. Today, we have collectively found the tools to apply pressure to institutions and individuals who are used to getting away with being oppressive. Goodbye to the days of public figures simply saying and doing whatever they want without facing some level of public intervention. Cancel culture isn't only about canceling people and places but also reminding the powerful that for every action there is a reaction—and that they can't control the narrative or its outcome.

For many years, cancel culture has been despised or misconstrued as a new phenomenon that's caused havoc on free expression and speech. We're supposed to now assume that we can't say or do anything without an angry mob instantly judging us and preparing to end our careers before they start. In actual fact, we are the people who make up the so-called mob, and we have control of our own actions.

As I've noted, before we were calling it *cancel culture*, society got caught up in the term *political correctness*. What started as an inside joke of a phrase in the late 1980s became all the rage within the media in the 1990s as political pundits and public figures began to bash the term in pop culture. You had personalities, such as Bill Maher, who branded his content as being "politically incorrect." President George H. W. Bush criticized it in commencement speeches, and even television shows like *Beavis and Butt-Head* were weighing in on it. The madness over the term would eventually inspire a 1995 book by John K. Wilson called *The Myth of Political Correctness*.

"A myth is not a falsehood. It doesn't mean it's a lie. It doesn't mean everything is fabricated. It means that it's a story," Wilson told NPR's Ari Shapiro during a July 2021 interview on the origins of political correctness.[4] "And so, what happened in the '90s is people, with political correctness, they took certain—sometimes true—anecdotes, and they created a web, a story, out of them, a myth that there was this vast repression of conservative voices."

The same thing is happening now with cancel culture: Powerful people are trying to suggest that they are being suppressed by the new ways that everyday people are reacting to their behavior. The notion of suppression is a myth: Those who fear cancel culture may claim they fear suppression, but it's accountability that they want to avoid at all costs. It's essential to ask the question of what, if anything, is being suppressed and why. When we hear critics of cancel culture either try to suggest that everyone makes mistakes or that cancel culture is an infringement on free speech, we should simply push back that no one's actual rights are being taken away. Cancel culture has never taken away anyone's rights; rather, it has publicly shamed people into reconsidering what they have decided to do with such freedoms.

The Dixie Chicks dealt with the backlash of conservatives who wanted them to repent for criticizing a sitting U.S. president. Powerful men in Hollywood who sexually harassed women were held accountable on social media, and sometimes these actions inspired criminal investigations. Whether or not the Chicks (as they're now known) or those predatory Hollywood execs felt the shame that was heaped on them is inconsequential. The effects of the shaming are consequential. Cancel culture is nonpartisan, individual, collective, religious, agnostic, political, and radical all at the same time. The act of canceling can be inspired by all these things without it being defined by them at the same time. History has shown us that those in power are obsessed with turning any form of accountability into a phenomenon that is intended to bring us into sudden doom. Just as political correctness morphed into "PC culture" that would later evolve into "callout culture," we are now seeing that the modes by which we are holding one accountable have never been new—but have evolved.

"I definitely view canceling people as more of a cultural practice than any sort of American political or discursive tradition," says Meredith D. Clark, who wrote an academic article[5] in 2020 titled "DRAG THEM: A Brief Etymology of So-Called 'Cancel Culture.'" "And I say that because American political discourse and political traditions are founded in and governed by white supremacy directly. And when I say that I mean to the literal exclusion of anyone who is not white, male, wealthy property owning."

While I take Clark's point about American history being grounded in white supremacy, I would argue that a cultural practice and a political practice are one and the same. And in the case of cancel culture—it is political *because* it is cultural. It's a tool used to shape culture.

Cancel culture is a way for a new generation of people to practice free speech. The way that we cancel today is more advanced because of our rights as a people and our access to digital communication tools. What opponents of cancel culture get wrong is the act itself: It's not *what* we're doing that's new; it's *how* we're canceling that's different. It's not the fault of the general public that society's more progressive than in previous decades. In fact, that should be the goal of a democracy. Perhaps the consequence of a more democratic or progressive society is for the most powerful recognize the limits of control they once had.

"It is a direct call to get better, do better, and be better for communities that are often marginalized," says activist/attorney Preston Mitchum on cancel culture's versatility. "Unfortunately, sometimes this must be done publicly to gain ongoing support and get the point across that what happened was unacceptable and for accountability to be achieved."

All manner of checks and balances have been a priority since America's birth. Even though a bunch of straight white men debated reducing their own power to own slaves, suppress women, and steal land, their beliefs about offering free speech to the voiceless would have the greatest impact of all. This is why those who make the case that cancel culture is unpatriotic and undemocratic put themselves in opposition to what inspired America in the first place. There is no way one can look at cancel culture and not see its evolution from the Boston Tea Party to the Dump Trump movement. Society's embracement of the public shaming of high-profile individuals and institutions was here long before Twitter came about. What has changed is the fact that the traditional media gatekeepers who were highly selective of who got to speak out are now being challenged. Today, anyone who has access to a mobile/digital device can be amplified within this lottery of social media virality.

It's important to remember exactly how the term *cancel culture* itself came to be and why society's understanding of it now must be reconsidered.

The very origins of the term *cancel culture* came from Black digital culture that took off and became a part of the mainstream. Today, we forget that the mere phrase to *cancel* someone came from the lips of a cast member of a hit Black reality television show. We forget that it was Black Twitter that coined the phrase that was first referenced from a Black cinema classic in the 1990s called *New Jack City*. Cultural appropriation would take cancel culture from a popular piece of Black online vernacular into a pop cultural sensation that's now treated as a dog whistle by politicians and world leaders. How it left the confines of Black culture and made it into the hands of the world's most powerful is a testament to how social media has transformed the scope of communication, for better or worse.

It's not so much *how* cancel culture is operating that

has confused people or upset them—but *what* it's being called. When *cancel culture* was appropriated from Black influencers on social media, what was once a sarcastic catchphrase became a serious term. Just like how *political correctness* was initially an inside joke that ran rampant, so has *cancel culture* taken off as a phrase. Once those in power got ahold of the term *cancel culture,* they attempted to redefine it as a pejorative phrase, stripping away its craftiness and mischaracterizing its intention. It's like any cool phrase that gets taken too seriously and blown out of proportion by a cranky, uptight parent who isn't hip to modernity—*cancel culture* was reframed and weaponized by those in power who were afraid of what it could truly represent.

Some suggest a rebranding. "In terms of cancel culture, I think it's misnamed," said famed host and actor LeVar Burton during an April 2021 interview[6] on *The View.* "That's a misnomer. I think we have a consequence culture, and that consequences are finally encompassing everybody in the society, whereas they haven't been ever in this country." Burton was right in his assessment of what society is currently doing in this wave of cancel culture and how it's showing "good signs that are happening in the culture right now." He further argued, "I think it has everything to do with a new awareness on people who were simply unaware of the real nature of life in this country for people who have been othered since this nation began."

I don't believe reframing *cancel culture* as *consequence*

culture is the answer. Rather than run away from the term *cancel culture,* we should embrace it. Instead of changing the name of cancel culture, we should set the record straight about what it really is. Calling cancel culture something more specific like *consequence culture* or even *accountability culture* just concedes to the most powerful trying to police the ways in which everyday people engage with them. Holding the most powerful people accountable is never going to be desirable or appealing to them. It's like paying taxes—whether you call it an *annual payment* or *compulsory financial charge,* it's still a sum of money being pulled out of your account by the IRS. Semantics often breeds sensitivity, and when we consider who's the most alarmed by the language surrounding cancel culture—it's always those who are experiencing the brunt of it.

To hell with their feelings—cancel culture is here to stay. There will never be a favorable way to describe accountability to those who directly or indirectly oppress others. While *consequence culture* might be more palatable, opponents will quickly find another way to deem it problematic. History has shown us that there's never going to be a proper or "politically correct" way to demand change from those who are invested in dictating our lives. Respectability politics will always make society, especially marginalized people, believe that they can be spared from harm if they only appeal to their oppressors in a particular way. It's simply not true. Whether one describes same-sex marriage as *marriage equality* or *love is love,* bigots will be mad. The current conversation on how to rename or reframe cancel culture is a distraction from its very intention.

The fact that people—both powerful and less so—have been put on notice that whatever move they make can now be checked, not only by the courts, law enforcement, or government but by the people, means cancel culture has essentially won the cultural wars. Although still rich and influential, the most powerful have now been humbled by the digital accessibility of everyday people whom they once could simply dismiss or silence. And increased civic engagement is even more available to the people.

For our society and democracy to evolve, we've needed new ways to further free speech, civic participation, and collective action. Whether it is as simple as the acceptance that people should be able to choose their own pronouns or thousands of Black women calling on the music industry to mute the platforms of one of its very own R&B singers, cancel culture has given a voice to the voiceless at a time when other aspects of our democracy have become threatened.

Today, the voting rights we once thought were protected are under attack. Republican leaders, bitter over the presidential cancellation of Donald Trump, now want to make it harder for marginalized communities to vote. Such bold acts of intimidation harken back to the Jim Crow era, when powerful white men threatened the freedoms of Black people. Now these acts are called out more publicly on social media, influencing everyday people to call on companies and other leaders to take a stand more boldly.

In April 2021, hundreds of Fortune 500 companies,[7] such as Apple, Amazon, and Facebook, signed on to a statement opposing "any discriminatory legislation" that would negatively impact people's ability to vote. "Regardless of our political affiliations," reads the statement, which ran as a two-page ad in *The New York Times* and *The Washington Post,* "we believe the very foundation of our electoral process rests upon the ability of each of us to cast our ballots for the candidates of our choice."

Such a surprisingly bold move from powerful companies would have never happened had it not been for the collective calls for accountability from many of their customers—everyday citizens who signed digital petitions, protested outside of state buildings, and used their social media platforms to shame a lack of response from those they held in high regard.

The potential for cancel culture is democracy uncensored and unchained. Society can never go back to the world before social media, progressive rights, and the ability for those once oppressed to ever be silenced again. We shall never forget those who came before us, who could only protest in the streets so that we could one day have the privilege to speak truth to power online. As I hope I've convinced you, cancel culture is ultimately a force for good. Rather than looking at cancel culture as a danger waiting right around every corner, we should embrace it as an opportunity. Despite how critics have tried to represent it, cancel culture is not cyberbullying or doxing. Cancel culture gives us the chance to engage in new and exciting ways—civically, culturally, and politically. What could we change in the world if we used cancel culture as the tool that it is? Answer: Choose a cause you care about and get involved. There's no longer a major barrier to civic participation, and you don't have to boil the ocean. Like all forms of protest, cancel culture can be cumulative. The segregation laws around buses didn't change the moment Rosa Parks sat down. It took 381 days of Black people refusing to take the Montgomery buses—and the Supreme Court to rule that their seating rules were discriminatory—for things to change. Rosa Parks made a single gesture and created a domino effect that resulted in change. The Stonewall riots inspired Pride parades around the world and in turn send the message of celebration, rather than suppression, to LGBTQIA people everywhere. What you do *can* matter. It's as simple, and as complicated, as that. Although there are still many more hurdles to overcome and social barriers to cross, the demand for accountability, just like our ability to cancel, will never die.

ACKNOWLEDGMENTS

X X X X

I would love to thank my literary agent Stephanie Winter, editor Cassidy Graham, editorial consultant Ceri Marsh, literary mentor Eric Smith, and the entire teams of P.S. Literary Agency and St. Martin's Press for making my dream of becoming a published author a reality.

I am tremendously grateful for Kenyette Tisha Barnes, Leslie Mac, Daniela Capistrano, Jon Pierre, William E. Ketchum, III, Michael Coard, Preston Mitchum, Randy Robinson, Dawn Ennis, J. Mase III, Dr. Meredith D. Clark, and Dr. Anthea Butler, for contributing your clarity, nuance, and voice to this book.

I must thank all my friends and family, but most importantly my husband, Barry, for encouraging me to pursue my passion of writing a book even when it felt impossible.

This book would not have been possible without all the often ignored Black and Brown LGBTQIA voices who are constantly marginalized and erased from history. May this book serve as a testament that your labor, sacrifice, and resilience continue to be seen and felt. Your compassion inspires me, and may we all continue to cancel the hate that we know will never win.

NOTES

X X X X

INTRODUCTION

1. "Former President Trump Addresses CPAC," C-SPAN video, 1:35:41, accessed April 4, 2022, https://www.c-span.org/video /?509084-1/president-trump-addresses-cpac.

2. Cleve R. Wootson Jr., "A Black R&B Artist Hoped Singing for Trump Would Build 'a Bridge.' It Derailed Her Career Instead," *Washington Post,* January 18, 2019.

3. Clyde McGrady, "The Strange Journey of 'Cancel,' from a Black-Culture Punchline to a White-Grievance Watchword," *Washington Post,* April 2, 2021.

4. Liat Kaplan, "My Year of Grief and Cancellation," *New York Times,* February 25, 2021.

5. Ernest Owens, "Black Twitter, Justin Timberlake and Free Speech: How Speaking My Mind Was an Act of Black Liberation," BET, June 30, 2016, https://www.bet.com/article/1f0zdg /black-twitter-justin-timberlake-and-free-speech.

6. Elizabeth Wellington, "Justin Timberlake's New Song Is About Philly Journalist Ernest Owens, Who Couldn't Care Less," *Philadelphia Inquirer,* February 2, 2018.

7. Ernest Owens, "Justin Timberlake Revealed His True Colors to Me Before the Britney Spears Documentary," Daily Beast, February 18, 2021, https://www.thedailybeast.com/justin -timberlake-revealed-his-true-colors-to-me-before-the-britney -spears-documentary.

8. Mensah M. Dean, "Philly Police Counterterrorism Unit Interrogated Journalist over Facebook Comment," *Philadelphia Inquirer,* October 11, 2018.

9. Ayal Feinberg, Regina Branton, and Valerie Martinez-Ebers, "Counties That Hosted a 2016 Trump Rally Saw a 226 Percent Increase in Hate Crimes," *Washington Post,* March 22, 2019.

10. Monica Anderson and Jingjing Jiang, "Teens, Social Media and Technology 2018," Pew Research Center, May 31, 2018, https://www.pewresearch.org/internet/2018/05/31/teens-social-media-technology-2018/.

11. Emily S. Rueb and Derrick Bryson Taylor, "Obama on Call-Out Culture: 'That's Not Activism,'" *New York Times*, October 31, 2019.

12. Ernest Owens, "Obama's Very Boomer View of 'Cancel Culture,'" *New York Times*, November 1, 2019.

13. J. K. Rowling, John McWhorter, Noam Chomsky, et al. "A Letter on Justice and Open Debate," *Harper's Magazine*, July 7, 2020, https://harpers.org/a-letter-on-justice-and-open-debate/.

14. Matt Walsh, "It's Time for the #MeToo Movement to End," Daily Wire, September 21, 2018, https://www.dailywire.com/news/walsh-its-time-me-too-movement-end-matt-walsh.

15. "The Problem with Cancel Culture-#BLAKADEMIK," YouTube video, 49:25, posted by Blakademik, September 27, 2020, https://youtu.be/qpjdJwYxlgw.

16. Aja Romano, "Dave Chappelle vs. Trans People vs. Netflix," Vox, October 14, 2021, https://www.vox.com/22722357/dave-chappelle-the-closer-netflix-backlash-controversy-transphobic.

17. Daniel Kreps, "Surprising No One, Joe Rogan Defends Dave Chappelle: 'His Jokes Are Just That: Jokes,'" *Rolling Stone*, October 20, 2021, https://www.rollingstone.com/tv/tv-news/joe-rogan-defends-dave-chappelle-the-closer-1244854/.

CANCEL CULTURE BEEN HERE

1. Louis Wise, "JAY-Z on Fame, Fortune, and Lockdown Life with Beyoncé and the Kids," *Times* (UK), April 24, 2021.

2. Lauren Shank, "Opinion: Social Media Is Overrun by Cancel Culture," *Liberty Champion*, September 14, 2020.

3. Shannon Ho, "Deep Reckoning or Fleeting Outrage? Cancel Culture's Complexity Proves a Double-Edged Sword," NBC News, July 21, 2019, https://www.nbcnews.com/pop-culture/viral/deep-reckoning-or-fleeting-outrage-cancel-culture-s-complexity-proves-n1031466.

4. Ramsay MacMullen, *Christianity and Paganism in the Fourth*

to Eighth Centuries (New Haven, CT: Yale University Press, 2000).

5. Frederick Douglass, *A Narrative of the Life of Frederick Douglass, an American Slave*, ed. Deborah E. McDowell (London: Oxford University Press, 2009).

6. "Sojourner Truth: Ain't I A Woman?," National Park Service, accessed April 4, 2022, https://www.nps.gov/articles/sojourner-truth.htm.

7. "Read Martin Luther King Jr.'s 'I Have a Dream' Speech in Its Entirety," NPR, January 18, 2010, https://www.npr.org/2010/01/18/122701268/i-have-a-dream-speech-in-its-entirety.

8. Sydney Scott, "Civil Rights Leader John Lewis Urges Young People to Vote and Get in 'Good Trouble,'" *Essence,* October 5, 2016, https://www.essence.com/news/john-lewis-urges-young-people-vote/.

9. Bill McGraw, "Henry Ford and the Jews, the Story Dearborn Didn't Want Told," Bridge Michigan, February 4, 2019, https://www.bridgemi.com/michigan-government/henry-ford-and-jews-story-dearborn-didnt-want-told.

10. Erin Blakemore, "How Mahatma Gandhi Changed the Face of Political Protest," *National Geographic,* September 27, 2019, https://www.nationalgeographic.com/culture/article/mahatma-gandhi-changed-political-protest.

11. Robert C. Byrd, Mary Sharon Hall, and Wendy Wolff. *The Senate, 1789-1989: Classic Speeches, 1830–1993* (Washington, DC: U.S. G.P.O., 1994).

12. "Witch Hunt Fears, Triggers, and Scapegoats," Salem Witch Museum, accessed April 4, 2022, https://salemwitchmuseum.com/witch-hunt/.

WHEN CANCELING WAS THE ONLY OPTION

1. "March for Our Lives Highlights: Students Protesting Guns Say 'Enough Is Enough,'" *New York Times,* March 24, 2018.

2. The New York Times Salma Hayek, "Harvey Weinstein Is My Monster Too," *New York Times,* December 13, 2017.

3. Mark Satta, "Masterpiece Cakeshop: A Hostile Interpretation of the Colorado Civil Rights Commission," Harvard

Civil Rights-Civil Liberties Law Review, accessed April 12, 2019, https://harvardcrcl.org/masterpiece-cakeshop-a-hostile-interpretation-of-the-colorado-civil-rights-commission/.

4. Pete Hammond, "TCM Puts Classic Films 'Breakfast at Tiffany's,' 'Tarzan,' 'Psycho,' 'GWTW' and More Under Microscope for Offensive Content," Deadline, March 5, 2021, https://deadline.com/2021/03/tcm-classic-films-breakfast-at-tiffanys-tarzan-psycho-gone-with-the-wind-offensive-content-1234706957/.

5. Tyler McCarthy, "Conan O'Brien, Sean Penn Discuss Cancel Culture Calling It 'Very Soviet' and 'Ludicrous,'" Fox News, July 7, 2021, https://www.foxnews.com/entertainment/conan-obrien-sean-penn-cancel-culture-soviet-ludicrous.

6. Maureen Downey, "Racist Tweets She Posted at 17 Cost Her a Dream Job at 27," Atlanta Journal-Constitution, March 27, 2021.

7. "READ: President Trump's Rose Garden Speech on Protest," CBS58, accessed April 4, 2022, https://www.cbs58.com/news/read-president-trumps-rose-garden-speech-on-protests.

8. "Antifa: Trump Says Group Will Be Designated 'Terrorist Organisation,'" BBC News, May 31, 2020, https://www.bbc.com/news/world-us-canada-52868295.

9. Jonathan Capehart, "Black Lives Matter and 'Antifa' Are Not the Same Thing," Washington Post, September 1, 2020.

10. Gwen Aviles and Brooke Sopelsa, "J.K. Rowling Faces Backlash After Tweeting Support for 'Transphobic' Researcher," NBC News, December 19, 2019, https://www.nbcnews.com/feature/nbc-out/j-k-rowling-faces-backlash-after-tweeting-support-transphobic-researcher-n1104971.

11. Oscar Winberg, "Insult Politics: Donald Trump, Right-Wing Populism, and Incendiary Language," European Journal of American Studies 12, no. 2 (summer 2017), https://doi.org/10.4000/ejas.12132.

WHEN PROGRESSIVES CANCEL

1. Ben Mathis-Lilley, "Andrew Cuomo Blames 'Cancel Culture' for Dozens of Accounts of Him Being a Lying, Obnoxious Creep," Slate, March 12, 2021, https://slate.com/news-and-politics

/2021/03/andrew-cuomo-wont-resign-blames-cancel-culture-for
-reports-hes-a-lying-obnoxious-creep.html.

2. Denise-Marie Ordway, "'Racially Conservative' Attitudes Led
   White Southerners to Leave Democratic Party," *Journalist's
   Resource*, October 25, 2018, https://journalistsresource.org
   /politics-and-government/racism-white-southerners-democrats
   -republicans/.

3. Anthony Niedwiecki, "Save Our Children: Overcoming the
   Narrative That Gays and Lesbians Are Harmful to Children,"
   SSRN, July 29, 2013, https://papers.ssrn.com/sol3/papers.cfm
   ?abstract_id=2302716.

4. Samantha Senda-Cook, "Fahrenheit 9/11's Purpose-Driven
   Agents: A Multipentadic Approach to Political Entertainment,"
   Journal of the Kenneth Burke Society 4, no. 2 (spring 2008),
   https://www.kbjournal.org/senda-cook.

5. Tony Kelso and Brian Cogan, *Encyclopedia of Politics, the
   Media, and Popular Culture* (Westport, CT: Greenwood Press,
   2009).

6. Adam Taylor, "Was #Kony2012 a Failure?," *Washington Post*,
   December 16, 2014.

7. Sandra E. Garcia, "The Woman Who Created #MeToo Long
   Before Hashtags," *New York Times*, October 20, 2017.

8. Audrey Carlsen, Maya Salam, Claire Cain Miller, Denise Lu,
   Ash Ngu, Jugal K. Patel, and Zach Wichter, "#MeToo Brought
   Down 201 Powerful Men. Nearly Half of Their Replacements
   Are Women," *New York Times*, October 23, 2018.

9. "A Community Word about Shaun King: #SitDownShaun-
   Concerned Community," *Medium*, February 8, 2019.

10. Alexandra Schwartz, "Monica Lewinsky and the Shame Game,"
    New Yorker, March 26, 2015.

11. Ryan Wilson, "Obama on Kaepernick Protest: 'I Want Ev-
    erybody to Listen to Each Other,'" CBS Sports, September
    29, 2016, https://www.cbssports.com/nfl/news/obama-on
    -kaepernick-protest-i-want-everybody-to-listen-to-each-other/.

WHEN CONSERVATIVES CANCEL

1. Zack Beauchamp, "Nick Sandmann, RNC Speaker and Cov-
   ington Catholic Video Star, Explained," Vox, August 25, 2020,

https://www.vox.com/2020/8/25/21400805/nick-sandmann-rnc
-covington-catholic-video-explainer.

2. Scott Wartman, "Nick Sandmann Addresses the Nation at the
   Republican National Convention: 'I Would Not Be Canceled,'"
   Cincinnati Enquirer, August 25, 2020.

3. Kenneth Womack and Kit O'Toole, eds., *Fandom and the
   Beatles: The Act You've Known for All These Years* (New York:
   Oxford University Press, 2021).

4. Jordan Runtagh, "When John Lennon's 'More Popular
   Than Jesus' Controversy Turned Ugly," *Rolling Stone,* July 29,
   2016.

5. Phyllis Schlafly, *A Choice Not an Echo: Updated and Expanded
   50th Anniversary Edition* (Washington, DC: Regnery Publishing, 2014).

6. Allan Bloom, *The Closing of the American Mind: How Higher
   Education Has Failed Democracy and Impoverished the Souls
   of Today's Students* (New York: Simon & Schuster, 2012).

7. Dinesh D'Souza, *Illiberal Education: The Politics of Race and
   Sex on Campus* (New York: Free Press, 1998).

8. Michael Ellison, "Tinky Winky Falls Foul of the Moral Majority," *Guardian,* February 11, 1999.

9. "Tinky Winky Defended," CBS News, February 23, 1999, https:
   //www.cbsnews.com/news/tinky-winky-defended/.

10. Jonah Goldberg, "Sex, Drugs, and Teletubbies; Learning from
    the Enemy," *National Review,* February 11, 1999.

11. Justin Wm. Moyer, "Starbucks 'Removed Christmas from Their
    Cups Because They Hate Jesus,' Christian Says in Viral Face-
    book Video," *Washington Post,* November 9, 2015.

12. Trudy Ring, "DNC Chair: GOP Obsessed with Mr. Potato
    Head, Not Real Issues," *Advocate,* April 29, 2021, https://www
    .advocate.com/politics/2021/4/29/dnc-chair-gop-obsessed-mr
    -potato-head-not-real-issues.

13. Michael S. Schmidt, Katie Benner, and Nicholas Fandos, "Matt
    Gaetz Is Said to Face Justice Dept. Inquiry over Sex with an
    Underage Girl," *New York Times,* March 30, 2021.

14. Anthea Butler, "Faith Could Bring Us Together. But Too Often It
    Divides Us," CNN, November 24, 2019, https://www.cnn.com

/2019/11/24/opinions/religion-race-politics-division-butler/index
.html.

15. Sam Dangremond, "Who Was the First Politician to Use 'Make
America Great Again' Anyway?," *Town & Country,* November
14, 2018, https://www.townandcountrymag.com/society/politics
/a25053571/donald-trump-make-america-great-again-slogan
-origin/.

16. Michelle Alexander, *The New Jim Crow (10th Anniversary
Edition): Mass Incarceration in the Age of Colorblindness* (New
York: New Press, 2020).

17. James Forman, *Locking Up Our Own: Crime and Punishment in Black America* (New York: Farrar, Straus and Giroux,
2017).

18. Naomi Murakawa, *The First Civil Right: How Liberals Built
Prison America* (Cary, NC: Oxford University Press, 2014).

19. Dan Zak, "On Drugs, Nancy Reagan Just Said No. On AIDS,
She Said Nothing," *Washington Post,* March 12, 2016.

20. Ronald J. Ostrow, "Casual Drug Users Should Be Shot, Gates
Says," *Los Angeles Times,* September 6, 1990.

21. Anthea Butler, "Many Evangelicals Support Donald Trump. It
Could Be Their Downfall," *Guardian,* November 1, 2016.

22. Anthea Butler, "White Evangelicals Love Trump and Aren't
Confused About Why. No One Should Be," NBC News,
September 27, 2019, https://www.nbcnews.com/think/opinion
/white-evangelicals-love-trump-aren-t-confused-about-why-no
-ncna1046826.

23. Anthea Butler, *White Evangelical Racism: The Politics of Morality in America* (Chapel Hill: University of North Carolina Press,
2021).

24. Melanie Bencosme, "Macy's Cuts Ties with Trump: 'No Tol-
erance for Discrimination,'" NBC News, July 1, 2015, https:
//www.nbcnews.com/news/latino/macy-s-cuts-ties-trump
-n385131.

25. Daniel Marans, "Conservative Pundit Shoots New York Times,
Brags About It on Twitter," HuffPost, December 5, 2015, https:
//www.huffpost.com/entry/erick-erickson-new-york-times-bullet
-holes_n_56634545e4b079b2818eef7e.

26. William Cummings, "Former KKK Leader David Duke Praises Trump for His 'Courage,'" *USA Today,* August 15, 2017.

27. Masha Gessen, "Why the Tree of Life Shooter Was Fixated on the Hebrew Immigrant Aid Society," *New Yorker,* October 27, 2018.

28. Rony Guldmann, "Conservative Claims of Cultural Oppression: The Nature and Origins of Conservaphobia." *SSRN Electronic Journal,* 2017. https://doi.org/10.2139/ssrn.2907830.

NOT ALL CANCELLATIONS ARE THE SAME

1. Celine Castronuovo, "Cheney on Trump: 'I Will Do Everything I Can' to Keep Him Away from the White House," *The Hill,* May 12, 2021, https://thehill.com/homenews/house/553063 -cheney-on-trump-i-will-do-everything-i-can-to-make-sure-he -gets-nowhere-near/.

2. Jim Newell, "The Jan. 6 Insurrection Takes Down Liz Cheney," Slate, May 12, 2021, https://slate.com/news-and-politics/2021 /05/rioters-win-liz-cheney-purged-house-republicans.html.

3. Justin Baragona, "Hannity Insists Liz Cheney Wasn't 'Canceled': She Was 'Fired' for Being 'Selfish,'" Daily Beast, May 13, 2021, https://www.thedailybeast.com/hannity-insists-liz-cheney-wasnt -canceled-but-was-fired-for-being-selfish.

4. Rebecca Shabad and Dartunorro Clark, "'We Need to Make a Change': McCarthy Backs Stefanik's Bid to Replace Cheney as GOP Conference Chair," NBC News, May 10, 2021, https: //www.nbcnews.com/politics/congress/mccarthy-backs-rep-elise -stefanik-s-bid-replace-cheney-gop-n1266817.

5. Brett Samuels, "Trump Celebrates Cheney Ouster: A 'Bitter, Horrible Human Being,'" *The Hill,* May 12, 2021, https: //thehill.com/homenews/administration/553062-trump -celebrates-cheney-ouster-i-look-forward-to-soon-watching-her -as/.

6. Danielle Zoellner, "Liz Cheney Says More Lawmakers Would Have Voted to Impeach Trump but 'Feared for Their Lives,'" *Independent,* May 15, 2021.

7. Andrew Leahey, "Flashback: The Dixie Chicks Are Ashamed of the President . . . Again," *Rolling Stone,* August 7, 2014, https://

www.rollingstone.com/music/music-country/flashback-the-dixie
-chicks-are-ashamed-of-the-president-again-80036/.

8. Andrew Dansby, "Haggard Backs the Chicks," *Rolling Stone,*
July 25, 2003, https://www.rollingstone.com/politics/politics
-news/haggard-backs-the-chicks-248125/.

9. Billboard Staff, "Everything That's Happened Since Morgan
Wallen Got Caught Saying the N-Word on Camera," *Billboard,*
March 10, 2022, https://www.billboard.com/music/country
/morgan-wallen-timeline-racial-slur-video-9587738/.

10. Jordan Valinsky, "Time Magazine Puts Christine Blasey Ford on
the Cover," CNN, October 4, 2018, https://www.cnn.com/2018
/10/04/media/time-cover-christine-blasey-ford/index.html.

11. David Brock, *The Real Anita Hill* (New York: Touchstone,
1994).

12. Howard Kurtz, "A Revisionist's Nightmare," *Washington Post,*
June 10, 1993.

13. Jane Mayer, "True Confessions," *New York Review of Books,*
June 27, 2002.

14. Tim Weiner, *Legacy of Ashes: The History of the CIA* (New
York: Random House, 2008).

CANCEL-CRY ME A RIVER

1. Steven Nelson, "Rep. Jim Jordan Asks Judiciary Chair Jerry Nadler for Hearing on 'Cancel Culture,'" *New York Post,* March
1, 2021.

2. Claire Sanford, "Josh Hawley 2021 CPAC Speech Transcript
February 26," *Rev,* February 26, 2021, https://www.rev.com
/blog/transcripts/josh-hawley-2021-cpac-speech-transcript
-february-26.

3. David Jackson, "Conservative Political Conference CPAC
Drops Speaker over Anti-Semitic Tweets," *USA Today,* February
23, 2021.

4. Jonathan Martin and Maggie Haberman, "Trump's Republican
Hit List at CPAC Is a Warning Shot to His Party," *New York
Times,* February 28, 2021.

5. Dan Kovalik, *Cancel This Book: The Progressive Case Against
Cancel Culture* (New York: Hot Books, 2021).

6. Allyson Chiu, "Letter Signed by J.K. Rowling, Noam Chomsky Warning of Stifled Free Speech Draws Mixed Reviews," *Washington Post,* July 8, 2020.

7. Emma Camp, "I Came to College Eager to Debate. I Found Self-Censorship Instead," *New York Times,* March 7, 2022.

8. Joseph Wulfsohn, "Bill Maher's Warning to the Left: Cancel Culture Is 'Real' and 'Coming to a Neighborhood Near You,'" Fox News, February 27, 2021, https://www.foxnews.com /entertainment/bill-maher-cancel-culture-gina-carano-chris -harrison.

9. Tania Ortiz, "Cancel Culture Gives a Toxic Power to People on the Internet," *Cougar Chronicle,* September 29, 2020.

10. Aja Romano, "What Is Cancel Culture? How the Concept Has Evolved to Mean Very Different Things to Different People," Vox, May 5, 2021, https://www.vox.com/culture/2019/12/30 /20879720/what-is-cancel-culture-explained-history-debate.

11. Jon Ronson, "How One Stupid Tweet Blew Up Justine Sacco's Life," *New York Times,* February 12, 2015.

12. Elisha Fieldstadt, "Christian Cooper Would Rather Talk About 'the Underlying Current of Racism' Than Amy Cooper," NBC News, May 28, 2020, https://www.nbcnews.com/news/us-news /christian-cooper-would-rather-talk-about-underlying-current -racism-amy-n1216576.

13. Lauren Weber, "Can You Be Fired for Bad Behavior Outside Work?," *Wall Street Journal* (eastern edition), July 25, 2020.

14. Marlow Stern, "The Crucifixion of Courtney Stodden," Daily Beast, May 10, 2021, https://www.thedailybeast.com/the -crucifixion-of-courtney-stodden.

15. Elisha Fieldstadt, "Chrissy Teigen Laments Being in 'Cancel Club,' Says She's 'Depressed,'" NBC News, July 15, 2021, https: //www.nbcnews.com/news/us-news/chrissy-teigen-laments-being -cancel-club-says-she-s-depressed-n1274033.

16. Vidal D'costa, "The Raging Issue of Twitter Cancel Culture," *Times of India* blog, September 23, 2020, https://timesofindia .indiatimes.com/readersblog/issues-today/the-raging-issue-of -twitter-cancel-culture-26382/.

17. Claire Sanford, "Ted Cruz 2021 CPAC Speech Transcript Febru-

ary 26," *Rev,* February 26, 2021, https://www.rev.com/blog
/transcripts/ted-cruz-2021-cpac-speech-transcript-february-26.

18. Shaparak Khorsandi, "Cancel Culture Is Ruining Comedy—It's Time to Stand-Up to It," *Independent,* May 25, 2021.

19. Bruce Haring, "Alec Baldwin Again Attacks Cancel Culture on Twitter: 'No Code. Just Destroy,'" *Deadline,* May 15, 2021, https://deadline.com/2021/05/alec-baldwin-attacks-cancel -culture-twitter-hilaria-baldwin-1234757367/.

20. Matteo Moschella and Wilson Wong, "Joe Rogan Criticized, Mocked After Saying Straight White Men Are Silenced by 'Woke' Culture," NBC News, May 18, 2021, https://www .nbcnews.com/news/us-news/joe-rogan-criticized-mocked-after -saying-straight-white-men-are-n1267801.

CANCEL CULTURE IS DEMOCRACY UNCHAINED

1. Tom Grater, "Matthew McConaughey Addresses Cancel Culture, Freedom of Speech & 'Illiberalism' in 'Good Morning Britain' Interview," Yahoo News, December 15, 2020, https://www .yahoo.com/entertainment/matthew-mcconaughey-addresses -cancel-culture-103240402.html.

2. Jennifer Hassan, "Piers Morgan Called Meghan 'Perfect Princess Material.' Then He Targeted Her with Relentless Attacks," *Washington Post,* March 10, 2021.

3. "Reno v. American Civil Liberties Union," Teaching American History, June 4, 2021, https://teachingamericanhistory.org /document/reno-v-american-civil-liberties-union/.

4. Ari Shapiro, "How Cancel Culture Became Politicized—Just like Political Correctness," NPR, July 9, 2021, https://www.npr .org/2021/07/09/1014744289/cancel-culture-debate-has-early -90s-roots-political-correctness.

5. Meredith D. Clark, "DRAG THEM: A Brief Etymology of So-Called 'Cancel Culture,'" *Communication and the Public 5,* nos. 3–4 (2020): 88–92.

6. Katherine Fung, "LeVar Burton Defends Cancel Culture, Says It Should Be Called 'Consequence Culture,'" *Newsweek,* April 26, 2021, https://www.newsweek.com/levar-burton-defends-cancel -culture-says-it-should-called-consequence-culture-1586506.

7. Judy Kurtz, "Hollywood Stars, Business Leaders Sign Open Letter Opposing New Voting Restrictions," *The Hill,* April 14, 2021, https://thehill.com/blogs/in-the-know/in-the-know /548170-hollywood-stars-business-leaders-sign-open-letter -opposing-new/.